Cost to Serve Analytics

Strategise for success: A practical roadmap for customer service efficiency

J.E. McNish

Cost to Serve Analytics

Strategise for success: A practical roadmap for customer service efficiency

© J. E. McNish 2024

Published by Aston Campbell Associates

British Library Cataloguing in Publication Data

A CIP record of this book is available from the British Library

ISBN 978-1-0686234-0-0

eISBN 978-1-0686234-1-7

First published 2024

Register for the latest updates at www.costtoserveanalytics.com

Cover designed by Getcovers

Typesetting by JK Digital

Pexels.com photographic image credits

Page 3, 11 and 73 by fauxels; Page 5 by Mikhail Nilov; Page 28 by Alena Darmel;

Page 31 by Andrea Piacquadio; Page 47 by RF._.studio

Dedicated to my parents and the pillars of strength who came before, and to inspiring future rising stars to shine even more.

As I begin sharing the insights contained in this book, I want to express my sincere gratitude to the people I have worked with while developing this approach and all who have contributed, advised and supported me throughout the writing and publishing process. Their valuable input and encouragement have been essential in shaping the content you are about to explore. It is with appreciation for their insights and guidance that I present this work, hoping it serves as a helpful resource for all who engage with it.

J. E. McNish

Who Needs This Book?

In today's fast-paced and competitive world, leaders in both the public and private sectors are constantly challenged to deliver more with fewer resources. Balancing cost-efficiency while maintaining high standards of service and performance becomes increasingly difficult, especially when cost reduction efforts are met with new rounds of similar challenges, year after year.

Cost-to-Serve Analytics offers a strategic approach to not only meet current cost challenges but also prepare for those ahead. It is a comprehensive framework of free-to-use tools that you control, designed to augment your organisation's internal workings in a way that continues to deliver benefits year after year. By adopting this approach, you can plan strategically, optimise resources, uncover the cost drivers for each product or service, improve decision-making, and drive sustainable growth—all without compromising quality or customer satisfaction.

This book is for anyone looking to move beyond intuition and guesswork and instead leverage data to make smarter, more informed decisions. Whether you're a senior executive responsible for budgeting and strategy, a team leader seeking to streamline operations, or someone focused on improving services, this book provides the tools, insights, and frameworks to maximise your organisation's efficiency and long-term value.

It will support your organisation to

- Maximise long-term gains
- Simplify complex operations
- Measure ROI clearly
- Achieve the delicate balance between cost efficiency and quality
- Prepare for future budget cuts
- Make data-driven decisions
- Plan strategically
- Mitigate risks effectively
- Future-proof your organisation

Contents

Navigation Map

Every reader's journey is unique. This map is designed to guide you directly to the content that meets your specific needs.

Curious About Cost-to-Serve?

- What is Cost-to-Serve? — Page 7
- Origins and Background — Section 1
- Cost-to-Serve Implementation FAQs — Section 1.1

Assessing Your Starting Point

- Where Are You Now? (Maturity Model) — Appendix 8.6
- Choosing Your Approach — Section 2.0

Building Your Business Case

- Questions to help Sponsors Keep the Project on Track — Sections 2.7 & 7.0
- Business Case Suggestions — Section 3

Planning a Cost-to-Serve Implementation

- Roles and Responsibilities — Section 3.7
- Guidance for Product Owners/Project Managers — Section 4.0
- Guidance for Workstream Leads — Section 5.0

Consolidating the Outputs

- Combining the Outputs — Section 6.0

Exploring Your Data

- Tips for Maximising Value from Your Data — Section 7.0

Real-World Examples

- Case Studies — Section 8.0

Foreword

There are various publications on activity based costing and cost to serve, but this one is geared towards empowering senior stakeholders to lead the initiative, project managers to implement it, and business managers to utilise cost to serve analytics capabilities to innovate, support, and inform decision making.

How often do you encounter cost-cutting measures that ultimately undermine customer satisfaction? This book is designed to support the systemic identification and quantification of end-to-end waste while advocating for cost transparency, streamlined processes, and customer experience design. By prioritising efficiency without compromising clarity in the customer journey, it benefits both customers and organisations alike. Reducing the need for customers to make contact ultimately increases satisfaction levels and drives down operational costs.

The background to this book began when Jacqui and I collaborated on a project that played a crucial role in shaping the initial versions of the Local Government Service List (LGSL). The LGSL serves as a comprehensive catalogue of the services that Local Government in England and Scotland provide to the public. The project's success led to an invitation from the then Improvement and Development Agency (IDeA), now known as the Local Government Association (LGA), to collaborate with other organisations in developing a unified list for England. The list was subsequently nationally adopted, received significant international interest, was used to benchmark progress on national and commercial agendas, and was adopted by the community and its partners.

In tandem, Jacqui led a project to assess costs associated with public-facing services provided by a large organisation, aligning services with the LGSL and customer profiles, and chaired the London region's eGovernment group. The group took a keen interest in the project outcomes. Subsequently, Jacqui facilitated collaboration among the partners Porism (a technology partner), the IDeA, and Experian (who contributed their Mosaic segmentation data). The program received partial funding from the Department of Communities and Local Government, with additional contributions from participating organisations. We both worked on the customer profiling project which, aligned with local objectives, benchmarked service delivery costs, access channel usage, and service take-up by access channel and segmented customer profiles. These experiences laid the groundwork for the work presented here.

The outcomes of this work (Aston Campbell Associates) are acknowledged and cited in various publications, including the 2009 HM Government document 'Putting the Frontline First: Smarter Government', the 'Champion for Digital Inclusion: The Economic Case for Digital Inclusion' report, the review of infrastructure in the public sector in Scotland, the Government Digital Efficiency report from November 2012, and presentations at events such as the Parliament and Internet Conference 2010 and Race Online 2012/PWC.

Since then, Jacqui has been actively involved in assisting organisations in understanding and optimising service delivery. This book encapsulates her experiences, providing a rationale for conducting cost to serve exercises and offering checklists of essential considerations. Intended as a practical guide, it aids in the application of theory, presenting templates, formulas, and examples for hands-on implementation.

Sheila Apicella, Assistant Director Local eGovernment Standards Body 2003–2004, Principal Consultant and Project Lead IDeA 2004–2007.

Why I wrote this book

Imagine being the conductor of an orchestra, not just appreciating the music, but possessing a deep understanding of each instrument, enabling you to harmonise their individual sounds and create mesmerising symphonies of innovation. This is what happened the first time I designed and completed the exercises contained in this manual, it fuelled imaginations, unlocked insights and released the potential for so much more.

Having an analytical edge is like owning a weapon that provides powerful advantage, fuelled by data-driven insights. It is about possessing the ability to extract meaningful conclusions from complex information, empowering smarter decisions and strategies. This edge allows one to uncover hidden patterns, foresee trends, and derive actionable solutions from the vast array of available data. It is not just about collecting information but transforming it into valuable knowledge that guides precision, efficiency, and innovation, setting the stage for impactful and informed leadership.

Having worked in a range of strategic transformational roles during my career, I recognised that without knowing the cost to serve, managers often have little choice but to make tough decisions when faced with making cuts, because the dashboards at their disposal have too few dials. Therefore, management may frequently decide on cuts without being able to estimate the impact on the overall business.

This book empowers organisations to project manage a cost to serve initiative from deliverables to benefits realisation, with support for quality and repeatability considered. It culminates with a balanced scorecard designed to give management more dashboard dials with which to make informed choices. Decisions that will have the biggest impact on efficiency savings, customer experiences and staff morale.

Cost to Serve Analytics is a practical manual designed to help large service organisations to track the cost of delivering each service. It addresses the never-ending need to reduce costs and enhance quality by demonstrating how to quantify the expenses associated with delivering each service. It provides leaders with guidance, KPIs, and dashboards, project managers with implementation guidance, and business managers with the insight necessary for making informed decisions related to service delivery.

I wrote this book because I could not find any publications that practically dealt with building a repository of cost-to-serve knowledge, from a service management perspective. This book is not designed to do the thinking for you, rather it is intended to help you think. I imagine that there are several ways one could approach this, and this is the one I used in 16 organisations. If it helps, you can change all or parts of this to suit your circumstances, as long as your approach and the assumptions made are robust, defendable, repeatable, auditable, and recorded.

This text approaches the subject through the lens of senior leadership and project management rather than traditional finance and accounting. It is set apart from other manufacturing-led approaches because it goes beyond theories, numbers, and financial metrics, to provide practical support for an organisation choosing to embed transaction analytics into business as usual. The approach is collaborative, customer-focused and strategic. More importantly, results that will provide an analytical edge can be achieved regardless of the maturity of your organisational infrastructure.

Without an understanding of the savings that can be achieved by getting things right the first time, reducing waste and streamlining processes, cost reduction exercises can result in kneejerk reactions, which impacts the organisation negatively in the longer term.

Cost to serve explained

'Knowing the cost of delivering each service in itself will not make an organisation great, but an inadequate or misleading finance system will keep one from becoming great, or worse yet cause it to fail.'

Adapted from Douglas T Hicks.

Cost-to-Serve is a method for uncovering the true cost of delivering products or services to customers. Unlike traditional cost accounting, it breaks costs down to their core components—assessing each activity and process involved in serving a customer. This detailed analysis reveals the actual cost of service delivery, offering insights that go beyond surface-level figures.

Think of the cost of providing a service like planning a road trip for a group of four. It is akin to calculating the expenses for fuel, food, drinks, and accommodation, and then dividing this total by four to determine the average financial contribution needed from each person (refer to section 1.3 for insights on how cost to serve can benefit your organisation).

Abel, Gertrude, Charles, and Sarah are the four vacationers in this analogy. They already have answers to crucial trip-related questions: why they are going, where they are going, when they are going, what they plan to do or achieve, and how they will reach their destination and return. It is likely that each of them embarked on the trip for collective and individual reasons. After the trip, they evaluate if they met their objectives, drawing lessons to enhance future planned trips (see section 3.3 for insights on what your organisation specifically aims to achieve).

Our travellers have varying needs, constraints, and motivations for the journey, impacting the cost drivers. For instance, Gertrude depends on a wheelchair, Sarah must attend an online work meeting at a set date and time, Charles desires a detour to a historic site not on the planned itinerary, and Abel requires nine hours of quality sleep nightly, ruling out night driving. Each requirement imposes constraints that may affect costs and experiences. While they may opt to split universal costs like hotels, fuel, and tolls

4

evenly, the individual cost is unlikely to be equal. The organiser needs to identify each holiday component to separate collectively shared costs from personal costs (see sections 5.2, 5.3, and 5.4 for cost components).

Our travellers carefully selected the quality of the hotels they stayed in, considering factors like location, accessibility, price, and comfort to secure the best deal (see section 4.14 for insights on agreeing to a data quality ranking system).

The travellers did not set a budget for meal expenses, due to the unpredictability of quality and price and the variability of personal choice. However, the group, being budget-conscious food enthusiasts, aimed to maximise meal quality and minimise costs. They researched restaurant menus, reviews, and prices in the areas they intended to visit close to mealtimes, resulting in an estimated saving of £325 (£81.25 per person) for the trip. This saving would not have been achieved without them making comparisons in advance between restaurant ratings, menus, and prices (see section 5.52 for insights on variable channel costs).

Post-trip, the group assessed whether they met their shared and individual objectives, they also analysed their expenses. Each of them incurred different costs: Sarah opted for upgraded hotel rooms; Abel paid for single malt whisky night caps; Charles spent more for additional tourist experiences; and Sarah chose set menus and tap water, to minimise her personal costs.

Our four travellers are scouts for a tour company. Armed with a comprehensive understanding of customer preferences, they prepared for scaling up. The subsequent year, the company organised groups of 250 people for the same journey at a fixed price covering basics, offering add-ons for interested participants. Utilising the metrics calculated during the journey, they negotiated optimal group discounts based on evidence gathered.

Thanks to the data collected during the scouting trip, the travel company surpassed their main competitor by undercutting prices and improving profit margins. They also delivered superior quality, including gourmet meals at a set price, enhancing the overall customer experience.

Section 1:
Making it work for your organisation

1.0 What is the cost to serve?

The cost to serve metric is designed to drive cost reduction and enhance value by systematically quantifying the expenses linked to service delivery. It empowers leaders with the capability to pinpoint, measure, and cost previously unseen wasteful processes, thus enabling informed and strategic business decisions rooted in efficiency and effectiveness.

Cost to serve originated via activity-based costing. The Chartered Institute of Management Accountants defines activity-based costing as an approach to pricing the activities related to resource consumption and delivering final outputs. The first recognised proponent for activity based costing was George Staubus in *Activity Costing and Input–Output Accounting* (1971), where he proposes the principle that "The performance of an activity may require many inputs … take the cost of using each into consideration in computing the standard unit costs of producing the activity output" and concludes that data must be current, based on standard operating efficiency, and should be complete, with inputs and outputs broken down to components that pertain to an object or activity, to facilitate decisions regarding trade-offs and substitutions.

Activity based costing (ABC) has its roots in manufacturing. Kaplan and Anderson enhanced the concept through several Harvard Business School cases and articles in the mid-1980s. In their 2007 book *Time-Driven Activity-Based Costing* they describe it as a simple and more powerful path to higher profits. They introduce the practical utilisation of human resources in recognition of the fact that human resources are rarely 100% utilised and a resource is often not utilised fully on a single process. This allows for the identification of unused or overextended resource capacity.

As Guerreriro, Rodigues Bio and Merschmann note in ('Cost to serve measurement and customer profitability analysis', International Journal of Logistics Management, 19/3/2008), "The term cost to serve has been used to describe customer service costs by several authors (Kaplan 1989, Cooper and Kaplan 1998, Braithwaite and Samakh 1998, and Kaplan and Narayanan 2001)". Cost to serve is positioned as the cost of the administrative, commercial, and logistic activities related to customer service delivery as measured through the ABC methodology.

The cost to serve is a measure of the total cost associated with providing a service to a customer. It describes the costs incurred to serve the customer, including the costs associated with producing, marketing, selling, and delivering the product or service, as well as costs associated with providing organisational infrastructure, customer support and handling returns. In his book *Activity Accounting: An Activity-Based Costing Approach* (1991), James Brimson discusses the product life cycle. He proposes that if a new product is successful, it yields returns which the business considers to be the norm and expectations are measured by this baseline. When competitors enter the market and/or the cost of production increases, the overall profit for the product is reduced. Companies naturally respond by seeking to reduce costs to maximise profits. With the not-for-profit sector, skills related to delivering a process increase as levels of professionalism go up and standards are introduced, some of them legislative. As a result, salaries grow, demand for the service increases and staffing becomes more tiered, with the requirement for distinct roles and areas and levels of expertise. When this happens, direct and indirect costs increase. The response to this cycle in the face of budget restrictions is cost reduction. Without an understanding of the waste in the system, cost reduction exercises can be short-term, kneejerk reactions, which might include:

- Universal reductions in budgets
- Freezing
  - recruitment
  - overtime and pay increases
  - non-essential travel
- Cutting back on research and development
- Cutting back on consultants in the middle of their assignments
- Letting go of highly paid but strategically important staff
- Downsizing
- Encouraging early retirement
- Redundancies
- Policing expenditure

However, these hastily implemented service cost reductions pose significant risks in the longer term, these include reduced capacity for improvement, diminished competitiveness, impaired strategic planning, letting go of expensive but essential knowledge and expertise, making savings that result in unintended consequences that lead to negative financial impacts elsewhere in the organisation, and alienating customers who may leave due to process breakdowns and lengthening wait times or, increase the amount of contact they make with the service. The knock-on effect is the opportunity cost from the potential value of benefits that are lost when a choice is made that deletes or reduces the organisation's capacity to operate flexibly, learn from the past, innovate, and plan strategically for the longer term.

If you have not measured your starting point to know when and where in the life cycle of a product or service costs begin to increase, you will not have a grip on your ability to control expenses or sustain your profits. Brimson proposes designing costs out of products, activities, and processes as a potential alternative to kneejerk cuts. To design the cost of waste out of a process, we first need to breakdown what the costs are. When we know the costs, we also know how much we will save from making changes and whether the savings are cashable.

ABC is typically an activity led by finance departments. Activities tend to focus on the cost allocation of production. Cost to serve however, extends beyond the production process to include distribution, sales, customer services and the overheads of providing these. While embedding cost to serve into financial systems is important for long-term sustainability, the exercise of determining the cost to serve has been and can be done without making changes to accounting systems. This book is aimed at business leaders, directors, and heads of departments from service industries who want an evidence-based approach to managing and controlling costs. Having gone through the exercise, customers have been known to use the lessons learnt to inform the reframing of their accounting functions.

The main difference between calculating costs for manufacturing organisations and service industries is that costs are attached to employee numbers instead of the number of products produced. Attaching costs to the manufacturing of products is often not suitable for environments where labour costs dominate:

a. for businesses that are reliant on employee expertise,

b. where the focus is workforce optimisation,

c. in situations where cost allocation becomes complex when tied to product count.

However, if you operate in a mixed environment, Case Study 2 in the appendix attaches cost to products produced.

Many factors contribute to the cost for an organisation to serve its customers, including the complexity of the product or service, the number of customers served, the level of customisation available, and the distribution channels used. Effective cost management strategies typically involve a combination of process improvements, technology investments, staff training, and customer segmentation to help businesses to understand their customers, manage their costs, and optimise their operations. In his book *Activity-Based Costing for Small and Mid-Sized Businesses*, Douglas T. Hicks shares that an accounting system that is based on ABC will not itself make an organisation great, but an inadequate or misleading system will keep one from becoming great, or worse yet cause it to fail.

Knowing the cost of providing each service is like planning a road trip for four people, where the planner calculates the cost of petrol, food, and lodgings and divides the total cost by four to arrive at the unit cost per person.

1.1 Cost to serve FAQs

Will cost to serve work with unreliable or missing data?

The cost to serve method offers guidance in situations where data reliability is compromised or missing, suggesting workarounds, and employing a data quality ranking system to assign a confidence rating to the generated outcomes.

Does the cost to serve deserve a place in my armoury?

While the cost to serve remains a fundamental metric, advancements in technology and evolving business models have introduced additional methods and technologies that complement or enhance its relevance. Here are a few notable ones:

Supply chain optimisation Optimising the supply chain can significantly impact the cost to serve. Complementary technologies such as demand forecasting, inventory management systems, and supply chain automation enable businesses to streamline their supply chains, reduce inventory carrying costs, improve order fulfilment, and enhance overall efficiency.

Process automation and robotics Automating repetitive tasks and processes can reduce labour costs, increase accuracy, and improve overall productivity. Robotic process automation (RPA) and artificial intelligence (AI) can be employed to automate various back-office functions, customer interactions, and elements of the manufacturing process, resulting in cost savings and improved service delivery.

Customer self-service and digital channels Providing self-service options to customers through digital channels can reduce service costs and improve customer satisfaction. Online portals, mobile apps, chatbots, and knowledge bases empower customers to access information, resolve issues, and place orders independently, reducing the need for costly human interventions.

Cloud computing and software-as-a-service (SaaS) Cloud-based technologies offer scalability, flexibility, and cost-effectiveness. By leveraging cloud infrastructure and utilising SaaS solutions, businesses can reduce upfront investment costs, scale resources as needed, and access advanced software functionalities without significant infrastructure outlay.

Data analytics and business intelligence Leveraging advanced analytics and business intelligence tools allows organisations to gain deeper insights into cost drivers, customer behaviour and their own operations. By analysing large volumes of data, businesses can identify cost-saving opportunities, optimise processes, and make data-driven decisions.

Internet of things (IoT) IoT devices and sensors enable businesses to collect real-time data on various aspects of their operations, including supply chain, logistics, equipment performance, and customer usage patterns. This data can be leveraged to optimise processes, reduce costs, and enhance decision-making.

Systems thinking A holistic approach to decision-making – cost to serve involves understanding the true cost of delivering products or services to customers. They both focus on the interconnections and interdependencies within systems. Systems thinking recognises how alterations in one segment can ripple throughout the entire system. Systems dynamics is a methodology within systems thinking that can be used in conjunction with the cost to serve to understand the causal relationships and feedback loops within a system through the creation of models that represent how different variables within a system interact and how changes in one variable affect others.

Using cost to serve modelling combined with some or all of the above is like extending the concept of the internet of things and creating an additional category that I call service transaction analytics. Just as a well-conducted orchestra harmonises diverse instruments to create a symphony, enterprise systems thinking based on cost to serve modelling orchestrates data analytics and business intelligence as its insightful conductor, supply chain optimisation as its synchronised rhythm, process automation and robotics as its efficient performers, customer self-service and digital channels as its seamless audience interaction, cloud computing and SaaS as its interconnected stage, and the internet of things and service transaction analytics as its instrumentation.

Together, they create a precise and harmonious symphony of cost optimisation, operational efficiency, and customer-centricity, maximising value and providing the foundations for innovation and competitive edge for businesses. Incorporating existing advancements alongside traditional cost to serve analysis can provide your business with an amplified understanding of operations and evidence to support strategic decision making. This method does not replace your accounting system, it restates the same data, adding operational relationships to effectively support decision making (Cokins, G. *Activity-Based Cost Management: An Executive's Guide* (2001)).

Artificial intelligence (AI) AI emerges as a potent tool with the potential to revolutionise various aspects of business. AI algorithms and robotic process automation can automate significant portions, if not the entirety, of processes. Its applications span from locating and transforming data to analysis and presentation. Furthermore, AI plays a crucial role in predicting future demand, advancing customer segmentation, detecting anomalies, and facilitating scenario-based 'what if' analysis.

1.2 The purpose of this book

This book serves as a catalyst for employing cost-to-serve analysis and leveraging its outputs to build a comprehensive analytics repository. It is designed to support leaders in both the public and private sectors who face the ongoing challenge of delivering more with fewer resources. By offering a clear, data-driven path that moves beyond intuition and guesswork, this book provides a robust framework of free-to-use tools and insights that can be tailored to fit your organisation's unique structure, ensuring long-term, sustainable benefits year after year.

If creating a cost-to-serve analytics repository is not the ultimate goal, the outputs from this exercise can serve as a stepping stone to unlocking the potential that placing feedback sensors across your organisation's activities will deliver. The possibilities from linking other datasets are limited only by ambition and imagination.

1.3 How could the cost to serve benefit your organisation?

Embarking on a cost to serve initiative requires a senior leader to make a decision – this section of the book is intended to support decision makers. Here we explore whether the benefits stack up for you. The tables below list some of the reasons why you might want to embark on a costing exercise. They have been categorised

in terms of the following areas of responsibility:

- Strategy
- Transformation / Projects & Programmes
- Finance
- Contact Centres
- Service Design
- Human Resources

This is the start of your rationale for proceeding – the exercise will provide information to inform the development of your business case. If, after completing it, you decide to proceed, a copy of the completed form can be used to frame the strategic intention. You may find it helpful to look at every role and tick all the statements that apply.

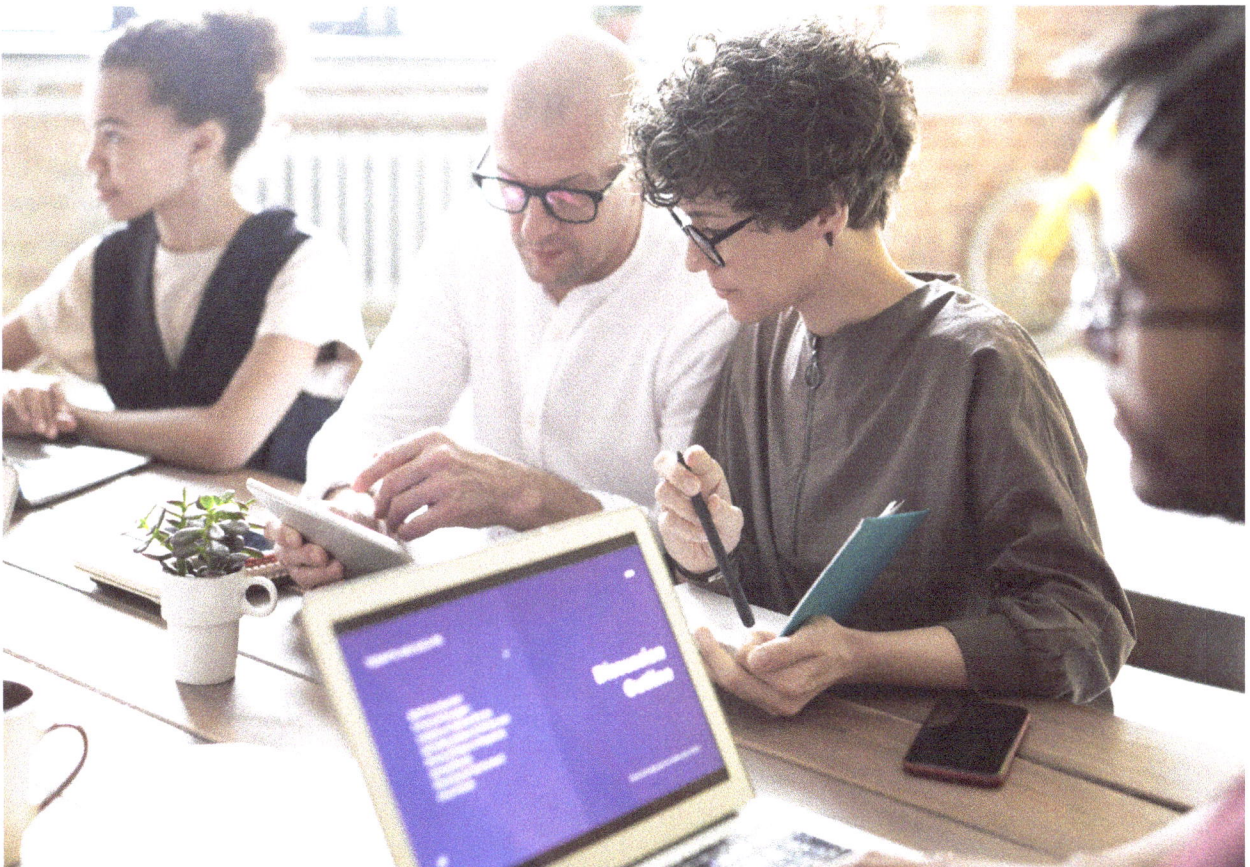

Strategy	Tick all that apply ☑
Enhanced decision support: To utilise CTS alongside a variety of decision support tools to to analyse past performance and assess the impacts of possible scenarios.	
Optimised resource allocation: To help the organisation to identify inefficiencies leading to better utilisation of resources, reduced waste, and improved value for stakeholders.	
Increased transparency: To increase visibility on how money is spent.	
Continuous improvement: Identifying areas for improvement, quantifying the potential benefits, and acting on these to improve and measure overall efficiency.	
Enhanced financial performance: Reducing the cost to serve for profitability and/or sustainability.	
Increased collaboration: To track the value chain of costs across departmental boundaries and partnerships to encourage deeper collaboration across silos, better coordination, improved outcomes, ownership of outcomes and increased efficiency.	
Strategic planning support: To identify areas where further investment could produce greater returns and to support the business case for developing a roadmap for future growth.	
Greater operational efficiency: To provide new data to support the streamlining of operations and increase efficiency, to improve productivity, reduce costs, and create a more agile and responsive organisation.	
Better data integration and/or customer insight enrichment: To enrich and contextualise data collection and integration to gain valuable insights informing competitive advantage and innovation.	
Time optimisation: Liberate your most knowledgeable resources from fire-fighting mode to future-creators who are fuelled by data-driven insights.	
Anticipating the impact of future budget reductions: To identify and address current operational inefficiencies to offer up savings that will not impact service availability or quality.	
Leveraging AI for business advantage: The metadata (data describing data) collected with the exercise will be used to provide the context for AI use cases aimed at automating all or parts of the CTS data gathering process, and to generate CTS insights, sense patterns and trends.	
Opportunity cost identification: To balance the trade-offs between dedicating staff to a single function and utilising them in more than one role.	
Evaluated intervention effectiveness: To compare the CTS from change interventions against a baseline.	
To mitigate risks:	

Transformation/Projects & Programmes	Tick all that apply ☑
Greater operational efficiency: To provide new data to support the streamlining of operations and increase efficiency, to improve productivity, reduce costs, and create a more agile and responsive organisation.	
Improved resource management: To provide insights into how efficiently the department is utilising resources and identify where improvements can be made and the impact the improvements are likely to have. To facilitate more informed and effective decision making about resource allocation.	
Improved service quality: To quantify and qualify the benefits of improving service quality, such as improving the customer journey, reducing wait times, improving the customer experience, and increasing the capture and accuracy of data that can be translated into insights.	
Cost savings: To identify opportunities for streamlining processes, reducing waste and failure demand, with the aim of improving financial performance to reinvest, repurpose, or to bank savings.	
Increased collaboration: To track costs across departmental boundaries and partnerships, encouraging deeper collaboration across silos, better coordination, improved outcomes, shared KPIs and increased efficiency.	
Evidenced benefits realisation: To compare pre and post optimisation performance using standard units of measurement across the organisation. Leading to evidenced outcomes such as cost reduction and benefits realisations in the form of cashable savings or redeployed resources.	
Reduction in failure demand: To identify and quantify the cost of failure demand and avoidable customer contact, and the return on investment (ROI) associated with eliminating root causes from the customer journey.	
Evaluated intervention effectiveness: To compare the CTS from change interventions against a baseline.	
To mitigate risks:	

Finance	Tick all that apply ☑
Better financial planning: To identify hidden inefficiencies to calculate the ROI from projects aimed at reducing revenue costs or increasing revenue income.	
Better understanding of cost drivers: To better identify and quantify previously obscured cause and effect cost drivers for various parts of the business, to support the development of more efficient cost models.	
Better risk management: To inform the development of more nuanced risk management strategies aimed at revealing the opportunity cost trade-offs involved in different financial decisions as they relate to business operations.	
More accurate financial reporting: To provide more accurate and reliable financial reports, aimed at compliance with regulatory requirements, and improved transparency for stakeholders.	
Data informed investment decisions: To identify areas of opportunity and areas of risk. A truer picture of the cost to serve can help inform decisions about where and when to invest or cut back.	
More accurate pricing strategies: To increase confidence and the accuracy of product pricing strategies.	

Contact Centres	Tick all that apply ☑
Tangible operational efficiency: To support the identification of inefficient service designs, communications, and processes, to support and measure the cost impact of continuous improvement efforts.	
Intangible operational efficiency: To identify areas where customer services can be improved, such as reducing wait times, improving first contact resolution rates, and/or increasing the accuracy of information provided to customers to support self-service and advocacy.	
Improved agent performance and resource allocation: To provide insights into how agents are performing, where improvements can be made and when and where resources might be better allocated. To use data insights to help the contact centre manager provide targeted training and coaching to improve agent performance.	
Achieved cost savings: To use the insight from the data generated to identify opportunities for eliminating waste, such as reducing call handling times, optimising staffing levels, or reducing agent turnover, and/or to improve financial performance, make savings or invest in other areas of the business.	
Enhanced operational decision-making: Providing the contact centre manager with data and insights to make informed decisions for improving the customer's omnichannel experience.	
Optimised staff utilisation: To identify, price and compare the opportunity cost from both over- and under-utilisation of the workforce, to facilitate efficient resource planning.	
Identified customer journey frustration points: To measure the time customers spend engaging with each service.	
Evaluated intervention effectiveness: To compare the CTS from change interventions against a baseline.	

Service Design	Tick all that apply ☑
Improved understanding of the customer journey: To design services aimed at delivering valuable insights into digital and non-digital customer journeys to make continuous improvements that reduce the need for customers to make avoidable contact.	
Better alignment with business goals: To embed KPIs in the customer journey that measure alignment with business goals and contribute to more effective service management.	
Improved collaboration: To encourage greater understanding of the inputs and outputs across departments and teams, and to develop relevant cross-team KPIs that support business goals.	
Achieved channel shift: To embed metrics that encourage customers who can do so, to use digital self-service channels by measuring the impact of effective signposting, against a baseline, and designing intuitive customer journeys.	
Enhanced customer segmentation: To divide a customer base into distinct groups or segments based on shared characteristics, behaviours, or preferences, in order to better understand how to measure the benefits of targeting, adoption, and providing personalised service offerings.	
Benchmarking: To benchmark service offerings with comparable processes, to understand differences, share lessons, identify best practice, explore the root cause of outlier metrics, and to support transparency.	
Leveraging AI for business advantage: To collect metadata with the cost to serve to provide the context for AI use cases aimed at automating all or parts of the CTS data gathering process, and/or to use AI to generate insights, sense patterns, and trends.	

Human Resources	Tick all that apply ☑
Increased productivity: To increase the average productive minutes available to the organisation by setting performance standards for workgroups.	
Improved workforce efficiency: To map average productive minutes to average transaction throughput and introduce a workforce efficiency metric based on employee experience or pay spine point.	
Staff allocation optimisation: To optimise human resource allocation.	
Staff incentivisation: As a component for incentive and reward schemes.	
Optimised performance management: To support performance management.	
Increased collaboration: To encourage organisation wide collaboration and the sharing of best practice.	
Communication transparency: As a mechanism for transparent employee communication and feedback.	

Your reasons

	☑
	☑
	☑

2.0 Exploring your organisation's cost to serve capacity

The cost to serve is like an iceberg, where the visible portion above the water represents the direct costs of production and delivery, while the larger, invisible portion below the water represents indirect costs such as marketing, customer service, and administrative expenses.

2.1 Depth and breadth

The type of cost to serve analysis you undertake hinges on the level of buy-in from stakeholders, the resources at your disposal, and the length of time the resources are allocated to the project. Here are four ways you might approach this.

1. Deep dive – fully cost the transactions within a scope that you define

2. Deep and broad – fully cost every transaction across the organisation

3. Shallow and broad – calculate average transaction costs across the organisation

4. Shallow and narrow – calculate average transaction costs for services within a given scope

You may wish to consider combining shallow and broad with data from staff surveys, customer feedback, and customer complaints to identify areas of the business where volumes and/or cost are high and customers and/or staff are unhappy. This approach will take less time, consume fewer project resources, and will identify the areas of the business where a deeper dive into the processes and culture is most likely to lead to solutions that will have the greatest impact.

If you choose to conduct a deep dive cost to serve analysis, you have the option to focus in-depth on a specific area or segment of your business operations. Deep and broad analysis will require similar resources to deep dive analysis since it will involve the same processes, the advantage being that it will create an organisation wide baseline and future standard for measuring and comparing all of your cost data over time. Shallow and broad analysis will provide average costs for services across the organisation based on transaction durations, it may not however fully take overhead expenses into account. A shallow and narrow cost to serve initiative will offer the same information as the shallow and broad approach but will be limited to providing costs for a particular service or group of related services. The information in the following table will help to inform your choice.

Depth and breadth of analysis summary	Tick ☑
2.1.1 Deep dive: This involves conducting a thorough examination of the cost components associated with each service or related group of services. It includes a comprehensive exploration of the average cost of a service transaction, encompassing all expenses from customer request to service delivery, while also accounting for overheads. For complex or multi-layered services it may include costing customer journey touchpoints. (This relates to any interaction or point of contact between a customer and a business throughout their entire journey or experience of using a service. By analysing touchpoints, businesses can gain insights into touchpoint costs, customer preferences, behaviours, and expectations at each stage of the journey.) A multidisciplinary project team will be required to execute this.	
2.1.2 Deep and broad: This involves conducting a thorough examination of the main cost components associated with every service and delivering a cost for each transaction type. It includes a comprehensive exploration of the average cost of a service transaction, encompassing all expenses from customer request to service delivery, while also accounting for overheads. This approach will require a multidisciplinary project team with members that are from more than one department. The team will be similar in size and skills for deep dive projects.	
2.1.3 Shallow and Broad: This method provides a simpler way to determine an organisation's transaction cost. Examination of each cost component is desirable, but not necessary. Shallow and broad analysis does not consider the duration of each transaction. This results in an average cost that is representative of all transactions within a group, thereby providing a cost for group transactions regardless of complexity or contact/processing durations. This approach will require less time, less staff, and less involvement with other departments.	
2.14 Shallow and Narrow: This method provides a simple and targeted way to calculate the average cost of a group of related transactions or transactions related to a specific department. Shallow and narrow analysis does not consider the duration of each transaction, resulting in an average cost that is representative of all transactions, regardless of their complexity or time requirements. This approach can be particularly valuable for projects that are limited to a specific area of an organisation; as a pilot, where time and resources are scarce; or if there is limited buy-in from other stakeholders to undertake a more comprehensive analysis.	

2.2 What can your organisation currently measure?

While (a) the annual cost of delivering services and (b) the total number of transactions per annum can help estimate the average cost to serve, there are several factors that cannot be measured with only a few data points. Some of these factors include:

- Variability in costs: The average cost to serve may not accurately reflect the actual cost of serving each individual transaction, as there may be significant variability in costs depending on the specific service or transaction. Without more detailed cost data, it will be difficult to estimate this variability.

- Complexity of services: Average costs may not fully capture differences in service complexity. This can have a significant impact on the cost to serve distribution curve, by including outliers that might have been excluded had they been separately identified and understood.

- Quality of service indicators: The total number of transactions per annum may not fully capture the quality of service being delivered. For example, if the service

is delivered inefficiently or with inferior quality. While there are other ways one could measure service quality, an unexpected spike in cost at any touchpoint of the customer journey or during processing will pinpoint where to focus efforts.

- Equitable outcomes for vulnerable customers: This might include tracking key metrics such as the percentage of service adjustments available as a proportion of the number of service offerings, the take-up of adjusted service access pathways, and the cost per transaction associated with utilising these alternative service access routes. Pathways might include accommodations such as braille, digital braille, large print, audio formats, easy read materials, translation services, British sign language support, validation processes for trusted intermediaries and live video support. By monitoring this type of metric, organisations can gauge the cost and effectiveness of their efforts in ensuring equitable access to services for vulnerable customer segments.

- Staff utilisation: The average cost to serve does not contain enough data points to identify services where staff are over- or under-utilised. This information offers numerous benefits, including optimal resource allocation and measurable performance improvement.

- Opportunity cost: Measuring the average cost to serve does not provide the data points necessary for comparing the value gained or lost when allocating staff time to one task versus the next best alternative or an optimal combination of the two. Measuring opportunity cost could also identify the tipping point where the time spent by skilled professionals on their own administration diminishes their productivity, resulting in lower unit production and potentially creating a backlog of unmet demand.

- Impact of external factors: The average cost to serve may not capture and will not differentiate the cost impact of external factors, such as changes in market conditions, regulatory requirements, or external service fulfilment charges.

The Cost-to-Serve Maturity Model in appendix 8.6 is intended to help you assess your organisation's current capabilities, identifying strengths and areas for improvement.

2.3 How deep is deep?

The annual cost of delivering services and the total number of transactions per annum can provide useful data points for estimating the average cost to serve. Additional data points will allow the organisation to further fine tune and optimise performance. Typically, the lowest data point is the service. With complex or multi-layered services, it may be useful to go beyond measuring the average cost of each service to include additional customer journey touchpoints, ie where the cost to serve is further broken down

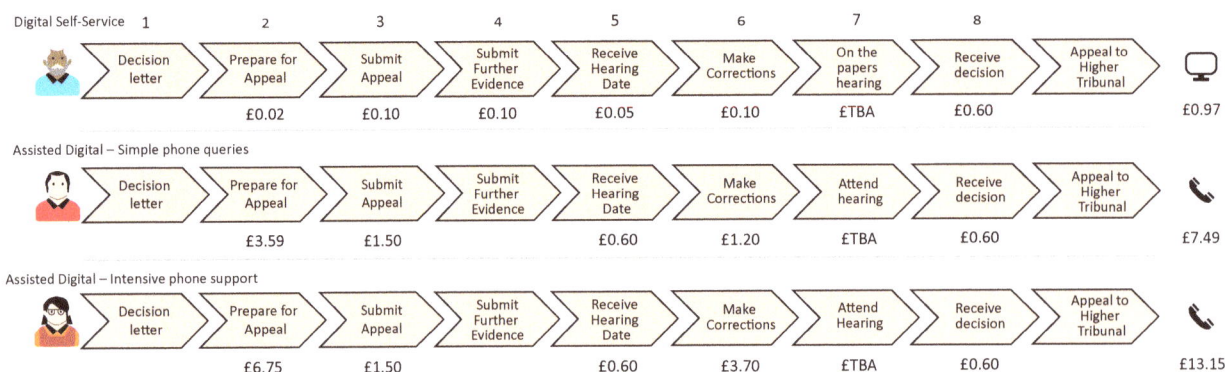

In the above example, segmentation based on digital capability was used to differentiate customers requiring digital assistance. This segmentation served as a focal point for user experience design. It was observed that approximately 40% of the digital self-service customer segment faced challenges when uploading documents. This insight directed the attention of the UX design team towards simplifying the document upload process for this group because the impact would result in significant savings for all but the most digitally excluded customer segments, who are transacting without the support of a digitally abled trusted intermediary.

Focusing on the simplification of document uploads was a strategic priority, as each successful instance of reducing contact related to uploads had the potential to save the organisation £1.50. By extending this efficiency improvement to all services incorporating document uploads, the cumulative impact becomes substantial, particularly for high-volume services.

By addressing the pain point of document uploads, the organisation sought to minimise customer frustration and, in turn, lower associated support costs. This aligned with the organisation's objective of providing an efficient, seamless, and user-friendly digital experience. Making targeted improvements to specific pain points within the customer journey helps to improve customer experiences and lower operational costs.

by the customer journey. This could be taken a step further by measuring the cost to serve by customer segment. In the example below, customers are segmented by digital capability to measure the omnichannel nature of customer interactions.

By using a deep dive approach to analysing the cost to serve at various touchpoints and across different customer segments, organisations can refine their service delivery, allocate resources more effectively, and design personalised experiences that meet specific customer needs. This approach enables a more nuanced understanding of costs and customer interactions, leading to improved performance optimisation and enhanced customer satisfaction.

2.4 Other operational cost savings

Where your organisation is pursuing other cost savings that are not covered by this book, please be reminded that these savings may be relevant to the calculation if you opt for deep and broad or deep dive cost to serve explorations. Examples

include changes to facilities management, accommodation, and technology costs. These changes should be factored into the calculations, and where they are not, finalised 'what if' scenarios should be employed. .

2.5 Decided to explore the possibilities?

Consider running an ideation workshop. Extend invitations to internal stakeholders and external experts, utilising tools like Edward de Bono's Six Thinking Hats.

2.6 Do not worry too much about the existing infrastructure

Ideally, your data infrastructure is advanced and capable of facilitating seamless data integration into a data repository, thereby enabling the automated generation of cost to serve figures for your dashboard. However, if this level of maturity has not yet been achieved, or if you operate in a mixed environment, you have two options: wait for the ideal conditions or initiate a baseline assessment now.

With the latter approach, a comprehensive exercise would be conducted annually, with the outcomes being utilised to inform change targets. Modifications to the cost base from subsequent change initiatives would be recorded in the dashboard and compared against the baseline. This can be achieved by mandating that project and programme boards overseeing initiatives encompassing technology, processes, property, and people must report on cost to serve KPIs. In addition, business unit managers may find it beneficial to use local performance information and monthly updates from the general ledger to track expenditure, commitments, and cost trajectories against targets. The information can also be used to plan for changes that would allow savings to become cashable in the future.

2.7 Senior stakeholder input into project/programme boards

It is advisable for the most senior leaders to communicate with the identified stakeholders to secure their cooperation for the project. A template for a suggested letter aimed at lowering resistance and increasing compliance can be found in Appendix 8.4.

In addition, senior stakeholders may find the following questions useful when chairing programme/project boards. The questions provide valuable steers for the current implementation and the scaffolding for future iterations of the exercise.

How does the exercise align with business strategy?

- Who is responsible for mapping the cost to serve into strategic business objectives?

- Who is responsible for developing KPIs and embedding them into the business?

- How can CTS be used to support decision making so that time, effort, cost, risks, dependencies, return on investment and the like are taken into account?

Who has been consulted?

- Is there a list of stakeholders for each area? True pictures can only be arrived at via stakeholder collaboration. With preparation, meetings and workshops need not be onerous or overly time consuming.

- Have the appropriate stakeholders been involved in determining the outcomes of the staff time proportion process?

What considerations have been given to audit controls?

- Is the audit documentation that records the approach regularly updated, does it use a standard format, is it stored in a designated place accessible to relevant stakeholders and are the processes and assumptions signed off by business owners?

- In considering making the exercise a precursor to automating the consistent elements of the cost to serve process to carry out defined tasks such extracting and/or manipulating data, has enough metadata been collected to map the necessary information?

How are you maintaining quality controls?

- Who is responsible for developing quality criteria?

- Are there existing boards with relevant stakeholders that could also serve as quality sign off boards?

- Is each data set accompanied by a data quality ranking?

- Is the quality ranking stored or is it being used in ways that would make it accessible for reporting purposes?

Who is the senior owner of the cost to serve project?

- Have process leads/owners for relevant parts of the business been identified?

- Is there a responsibility assignment matrix like RASCI (which identifies who is responsible, accountable, supportive, consulted, and informed), and if there is, how is it used?

- Who will own the cost to serve exercise for each business area post project and, how will this be managed?

How are we ensuring that the results will be embedded in business as usual?

- What role will have overall responsibility for cost to serve in the organisation?

- What board(s) will the initiative report into?

- What departmental roles and processes will be responsible for inputting to the data model post project?

- Who will be required to use the outputs? When, why, and how?

- How will outputs be incorporated into local and corporate KPI measurements?

- How will benefits be measured, who will ensure that the impacts from modifications to the customer journey are captured, analysed, actioned where necessary, and periodically reported? Metrics might include updated service costs, significant shifts in customer demand, and shifts in customer behaviour, including transference of demand elsewhere.

- What will be the triggers for feeding data into the model?

- Will the design of the dashboard support intervention analysis to measure the impact of an intervention or, treatment on a system or process?

- How can we use cost to serve as a strategic tool going forward?

Pitfalls to avoid

- How can you ensure that there is not a single point of failure for collating and analysing data, maintaining the dashboard, and delivering new dashboard features?

- Have you captured a full year's cost data by using the latest closed statement of accounts to measure the initial baseline costs against?

- Who is responsible for instituting and effectively managing periodic checkpoints, after making changes to the customer journey? These checkpoints will assess the new service costs and analyse shifts in customer behaviour, including demand transference to other service areas and changes in customer demand.

- How can we design a dashboard or reporting system that takes information access rights into account?

Refer to sections 6.1, and chapter 7, for further insights on effectively spearheading the CTS initiative within your organisation.

Getting started

There are a couple of important steps to consider:

1. Select a suitably empowered project sponsor

2. Appoint a visionary individual or team to spearhead the development of the business case and/or launch the project

The project manager will play a vital role in articulating the rationale, benefits, and feasibility of the endeavour. Additionally, to frame the objectives, they will require access to a copy of the choices you have selected above. This book will serve as a valuable reference, providing context, processes, and documentation to support their efforts in shaping the project's direction.

3.0 Business case considerations

Going back to our road trip metaphor. The four people would already have answers to the question: what are you getting out of the trip? They will know why they are going, where they are going, what they are going to do, see or achieve, who they are going with, and how they will travel to and from their destination.

Your organisation will have its own governance, project, and programme management infrastructure and you will have your own way of calculating costs. If your existing process achieves the same objectives outlined in this manual, and you have confidence that your approach is defendable, repeatable, and meets or exceeds the minimum criteria suggested here, then retain your process and use this manual as a checklist and to guide any parts of the process that may not be robust.

What are you trying to achieve?

It may be helpful to do this exercise with stakeholders who need to support the project or will benefit from the change. Use the information provided by the project sponsor and your own knowledge of the organisation to answer these questions:

- What new capability do you hope to deliver?
- What are the issues you are aiming to resolve?

- How will knowing the cost to serve help to resolve these issues or deliver new capabilities?

Describe the problem to which you would like to apply cost to serve modelling. In doing so, consider the following.

1. SMART goals: Focus on creating goals that are Specific, Measurable, Achievable, Relevant, and Time-bound.

2. Focus on outcomes: Consider what the desired outcomes or results of your efforts should be.

3. Determine which goals are most important and prioritise them accordingly.

4. Think long-term – think sustainability: Consider the broader, long-term impact of your goals and how they fit into or influence your overall vision.

5. Think about how you will evaluate progress, what will you measure? Think baselines, checkpoints, KPIs and consider the quality controls that may need to be in place.

6. Be flexible: Stay open to adjusting your goals as needed based on changes in circumstances or updated information.

3.1 Opportunity costs

Opportunity cost refers to the value of the next best alternative that is forgone when a decision is implemented. It is the cost of choosing one option over another. When a choice is made, the potential benefit from the next best alternative is the opportunity cost.

For instance, you may have the option of either recruiting temporary administration staff to fill a capacity gap or using more expensive skilled resources to fill the shortfall because they will hit the ground running. It is not just about the monetary impact but also the value of the foregone alternative in terms of reducing the organisation's capacity to deliver units of skilled labour. One of the calculations that could be factored into the exercise is the potential opportunity lost from increasing admin capacity and reducing the capacity to deliver the benefits, or utility that could have been gained. Understanding opportunity cost is crucial in decision making, as it helps in assessing trade-offs and making informed choices based on what is sacrificed by choosing one option over another.

Including opportunity cost data points with cost to serve data collections will support the following:

Benefit comparisons: To calculate the gain or loss from the returns of the chosen option with the benefits of the next best alternative. The difference between these benefits represents the opportunity cost.

Financial analysis: To compare the returns or potential gains from different investment choices. For example, if you invest in Option A and forego Option B, the difference in returns between the two represents the opportunity cost.

Staff time calculations: To compare the cost of the time spent on one activity versus the potential gain or benefit from an alternative use of that time.

Staff time optimisation scenario planning: To facilitate the creation of a 'what if' scenario interface aimed at optimising the allocation of staff time, to answer questions like: What if instead of hiring additional staff for areas experiencing high demand, we explore the possibility of deploying personnel with comparable skill sets from different organisational areas, to address fluctuations in workloads occurring at distinctly different times? What if we could determine the tipping point where skilled professionals manage their administrative tasks without impacting productivity or morale? What could be the cost benefit from scenarios such as streamlining processes, or automating certain aspects of the administrative workflow?

3.2 Wider benefits

A cost to serve initiative will provide your organisation with a strategic optimisation capability, which should be a consideration for the business case. Having an analytical edge means wielding a sharp advantage fuelled by data-driven insights. It is about possessing the ability to extract meaningful conclusions from complex information, empowering smarter decisions and strategies. This edge allows one to uncover hidden patterns, foresee trends, mitigate risks, and derive actionable solutions from the vast array of available data. It is not just about collecting information but transforming it into valuable knowledge that guides precision, efficiency, risk mitigation and innovation, setting the stage for impactful and informed leadership.

The return on investment (ROI) for a Cost to Serve initiative is both qualitative and quantitative. Qualitative because it captures the narrative behind the numbers, fosters cross-silo collaboration, and provides the organisation with deeper self-awareness, potentially fuelling competitive advantage. Quantitative because it measures the direction of progress, identifies tipping points, and provides the evidence base for strategically guiding the organisation. This includes cost control, performance benchmarks, optimised processes and resources, predictive budgeting and forecasting capabilities, and the establishment of meaningful KPIs.

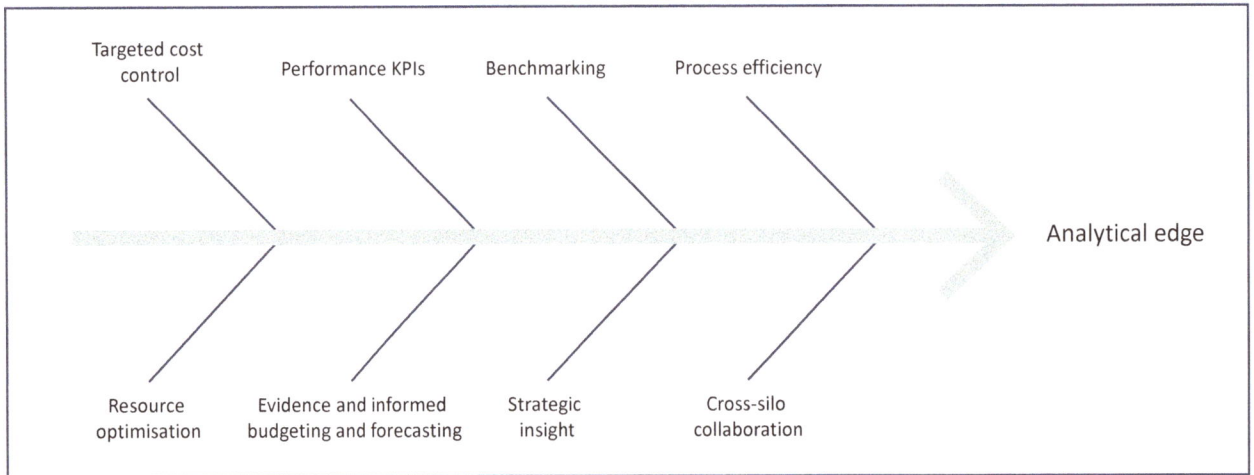

3.3 Categorising the benefits of the cost to serve for your organisation

Our four travellers will be embarking on the road trip for one or more reasons. Naming the reasons is them stating what they will get individually and collectively from going on the trip.

Start by ensuring that your choices tie in with corporate strategies or inform the development of new ones. Here are some reasons you may have for embarking on a cost to serve exercise. Use the following pages to record/articulate your own reasons: your business case for change.

Use MOSCOW Prioritisation

MO –Must have   S- Should have

CO – Could have   W – Won't have

	What will you be able to do that you cannot do now?	✓	Who will own it	How essential is it (MOSCOW)	Reporting/refresh frequencies
1.	To establish baseline costs based on a varying number of factors that contribute towards overall costs	✓		Must have	Quarterly
2.	To set up and report on cost related performance indicators, presented via a series of dashboards				
3.	To enable managers to drill down into a service to view the factors affecting the efficiency of delivering that service				
4.	To identify failure demand generated by customers who make contact because the process has broken down, they are confused, frustrated, mistrust the process, or are otherwise dissatisfied				
5.	To identify savings to map against future cuts				
6.	To measure post project cost benefits against baselines				
7.	To forecast using 'what if' scenarios and/or predictive analytics to identify potential savings and benefits that could be realised via process improvement				
8.	To design and cost accessible access to services				
9.	To increase the average productive minutes available to the organisation				
10.	To inform channel shift				
11.	As a user experience design tool to attach cost implications to service design scenarios				
12.	To add cost modelling to a customer segmentation toolkit				
13.	To use evidence to inform business cases for continuous improvement interventions				
14.	To support priorities and/or inform targets				
15.	For budgeting and forecasting				
16.	To develop new KPIs				
17.	To support LEAN value stream mapping				
18.	To cost behavioural nudging A/B testing pathways				
19.	To inform and evidence the impact of marketing initiatives				
20	To map average productive minutes to average transaction throughput				

3.4 Who will use the outputs and how will they be used?

	What will you be able to do that you cannot do now?	Who will own it?	Who will use it?	How essential is it (MOSCOW)?	How frequently should it be reported and how will you embed reporting into business as usual?

3.5 List of business units and departments in scope

List the front-line departments you wish to include within the scope here.

1.

2.

3.

4.

5.

3.6 Establish the project scope

Having identified the business units in scope, you will need to decide how deep and broad the scope will be for each department. Use the following table to help you decide. It may be helpful to name the stakeholders responsible for securing access or providing quality assurance for the calculations. Please refer to 2.1 for definitions.

Component	Deep and broad – entire organisation	Deep dive – selected areas	Shallow and broad – entire organisation	Shallow and narrow – selected areas	Hybrid (you choose)
1. Full time equivalent staff (FTE) count for the service	✓	✓			✓
2. Annual transaction volumes (customer contacts/requests)	✓	✓	✓	✓	✓
3 Average transaction contact minutes	✓	✓	✓	✓	
4 Average wrap up minutes per contact	✓	✓	✓	✓	
5 Average processing time (back-office staff)	✓	✓			
6 Average fulfilment cost per transaction	✓	✓	✓	✓	
7 Annual front-office contact minutes	✓	✓			
8 Annual back-office contact minutes	✓	✓			
9 Annual fixed channel costs	✓	✓			
10. Annual variable channel costs	✓	✓			
11. Average salary per FTE	✓	✓	✓	✓	✓
12. Property cost per FTE	✓	✓			
13. Direct employee costs per FTE per business unit	✓	✓			
14. Indirect employee cost per FTE per business unit	✓	✓			
15. On-costs per FTE	✓	✓			
16. Assumed staff utilisation per service.	✓	✓			
17. Average annual productive minutes per FTE	✓	✓	✓	✓	✓
18. Wait time and transportation costs/time	✓	✓			

3.7 Roles and responsibilities

Clearly defined roles and responsibilities are essential for both pre- and post-project phases. They provide several key benefits, including clarity, accountability, support, effective communication, and project success.

A tool for delineating these roles and responsibilities is RASCI, an acronym that stands for the following:

- **Responsible (R):** These are the individuals personally responsible for executing a specific task or activity.

- **Accountable (A):** The accountable person is answerable for the task's success or failure. They ensure that the responsible party performs the task effectively.

- **Support (S):** The support category includes individuals or teams who assist the responsible party in completing the task by providing necessary resources, information, or support.

- **Consult (C):** Consult pertains to people who are consulted for their expertise or input before the task is executed. Their opinions and insights are valuable for the task's success.

- **Inform (I):** Inform refers to stakeholders or individuals who need to be kept informed about the task's progress and completion. They are updated on the task's status.

While RASCI is considered a best practice in project management, it is equally important for stakeholders to extend this framework beyond the project phase. Ensuring ownership and clearly defined responsibilities post project is crucial for long-term success.

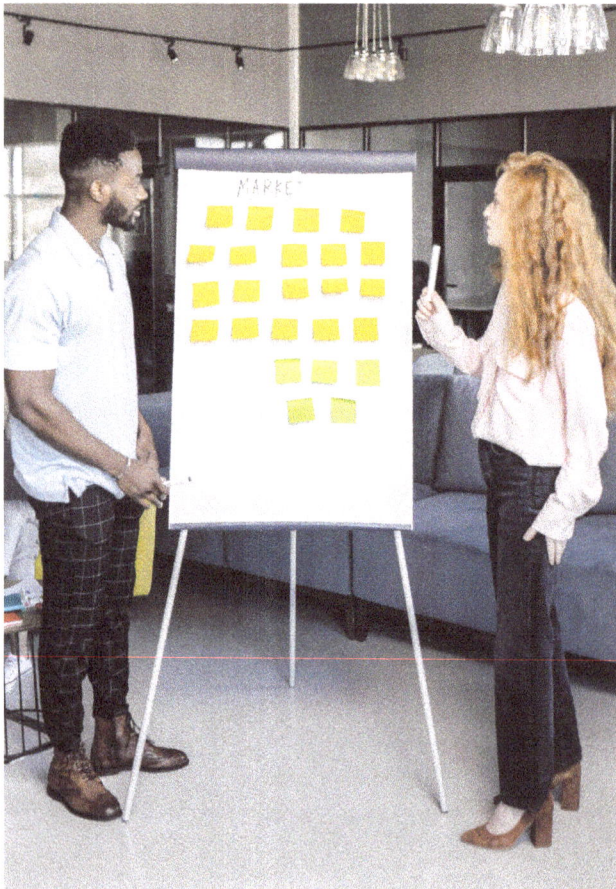

Section 2:

29

Managing the project

4.0 Project guidance

The project manager will oversee and coordinate initiatives aimed at understanding and optimising the costs associated with delivering products or services to customers. They will use the guidance on strategic intent and the scope provided by the project sponsor. The role involves shaping project objectives, ensuring governance structures are in place, identifying and managing resources, overseeing data analysis, and identifying and presenting cost-saving strategies. This guidance is not intended to change the way you or your organisation approaches projects, but to support you on the journey.

The road trip party did not set a strict budget for meals on the go, recognising that this is a variable that cannot be fully controlled. However, as food enthusiasts on a budget, they aimed to maximise meal quality while minimising costs. By researching menus, reviews, and prices for restaurants in the areas they anticipated being near at specific times of the day, they discovered that price ranges varied by an average of £25 per person. By selecting their dining options in advance, they estimated a total savings of £325 for the entire trip—a saving that would not have been possible without this prior research.

Optional data requirements can wield a comparable influence. Each unit of measurement functions akin to a touchpoint sensor. As a service offering becomes more granularly delineated (e.g. applying, status chasing, complaining), it not only expands reporting possibilities but also enhances precision in decision-making capabilities.

4.1 Prerequisites

4.1.1 Appointing a cost centre lead

Cost centres play a crucial role in cost calculation as they allow the organisation to organise expenses based on different activities. The accuracy and reliability of the financial data assigned to a cost centre depends on being able to reliably allocate cost centre hierarchies to departments and business units. Where cost allocations are unclear, collaborations with the budget holder may be necessary to determine the formula for allocating costs. The rules applied will need to be documented to ensure that the process is repeatable.

4.1.2 Appointing sponsors or boards for data quality sign-off

Data quality custodians play a crucial role in ensuring the model is fed with reliable data. They are responsible for ensuring data joins follow business rules, confirming completeness (which may require annualising incomplete data sets), and ensuring that data can be captured in the same way repeatably. More specifically, their role involves a deep understanding of the data, focusing on compliance, validating assumptions, and assigning data quality rankings.

4.1.3 Managing process flows across departmental silos

In situations where processes involve multiple teams (such as front-office, back-office, and finance) or are high in volume or value, and it is unclear how to effectively track the flow of customer transactions across these business silos, it may be beneficial to appoint an owner responsible for the end-to-end process. The product owner would be responsible for ensuring that a front-office process aligns with a corresponding process in the back office. For this role to be effective, the project process owner would require senior stakeholder support. Responsibilities would include facilitating collaboration across departments to map transaction workflows, specifically focusing on staff contact times by job grade. Where contact times are not captured automatically, they can be recorded manually over a defined period and then extrapolated for analysis.

4.1.4 Agreeing a data quality ranking system

Decide on the period for your cost to serve exercise so that the data sets collated relate to the same time frame. Annual data is ideal because it benefits from capturing periodic trends. However, other units of time can be used and annualised so that the data can be expressed in terms of an annual value.

Abel, Gertrude, Charles, and Sarah will have decided on the quality of accommodation that they will be staying in. They will consider numerous factors, such as price, comfort, or a balance between the two, to secure the best possible comfort at the most affordable price. The same considerations are required for data.

Because decisions will be made based on the outcome of this exercise, a confidence rating should be attached to each data element. The rating should follow the data element through the calculation to ensure that confidence can be considered when decisions are being made.

Giving each data element a confidence rating provides a visual indication of reliability. The overall rating for any given element of data will be the average ranking of all its data components.

Data quality ranking	Description	Data quality requirements	Requirements for customer segmentation
★★★★★ 5 Stars – Excellent	A reliable representation of annual volumes and contact or processing durations where collection is automated and not subject to human validation or interpretation.	Annual transaction data containing service names or transaction reason, transaction volumes, transaction date and transaction duration. Examples include switch data from phone lines, data from automated telephone payment systems and web payments.	Transaction records include the customer's full postcode/zip code.
★★★★ 4 Stars –Good	Data represents six months or more of transaction records which may have been subject to a limited level of manipulation and interpretation to extract and/or attain annual figures.	Annual or annualised transaction records containing service names or transaction reason, transaction date and time, and transaction duration.	Transaction records include the customer's full postcode/zip code.
★★★ 3 Stars - Satisfactory	Data represents three months or more of transaction records with contact durations, where there may be gaps or inaccurate use of telephone transaction wrap up codes.	Annual or annualised transaction data containing service names or transaction reason, transaction volumes, transaction date and transaction duration. Examples include data entry system reports from CRMs or ticketing systems.	Transaction records include the customer's full postcode/zip code.
★★ 2 Stars –Fair	Service metrics based on previous analysis. This is information collected from projects, performance indicators, and research conducted within the previous two years.	Annualised data containing service names or transaction reason, transaction volumes, transaction dates or periods and average transaction duration.	It is unlikely that this data will contain transaction postcodes/zip codes.
★ 1 Star –Poor	This data's reliability and representativeness is hugely limited and should be included for completeness with caveats.	11- or 2-weeks' worth of tick sheet data used for annual assumptions or staff estimates about volumes and durations or estimates from one department applied to another not dissimilar department.	It is unlikely that this data will contain transaction postcodes/zip codes.

4.1.5 Setting data collection standards

An important part of arriving at the cost to serve is ensuring that data and metadata are collected and processed in a consistent way: standard service name identifiers will enable data from various sources to be joined; collecting post/ zip codes of customers enables geographic analysis; uniform date and time formats ensure consistency in tracking and analysing time-based metrics. The implementation of standards serves as the foundation for accurate, repeatable, and meaningful data and allows cost to serve data to be comparable over time. The high-level diagram below suggests the data flows that you may wish to consider. You are encouraged to construct your own.

4.1.6 Selecting the data analysis and cost centre leads

Individuals in these positions must possess both visionary thinking and practical expertise, enabling them to envision innovative solutions and execute them effectively. The right leaders will understand the challenge and develop tailored local requirements without relying on detailed, step-by-step instructions.

Suggesting data mapping requirements

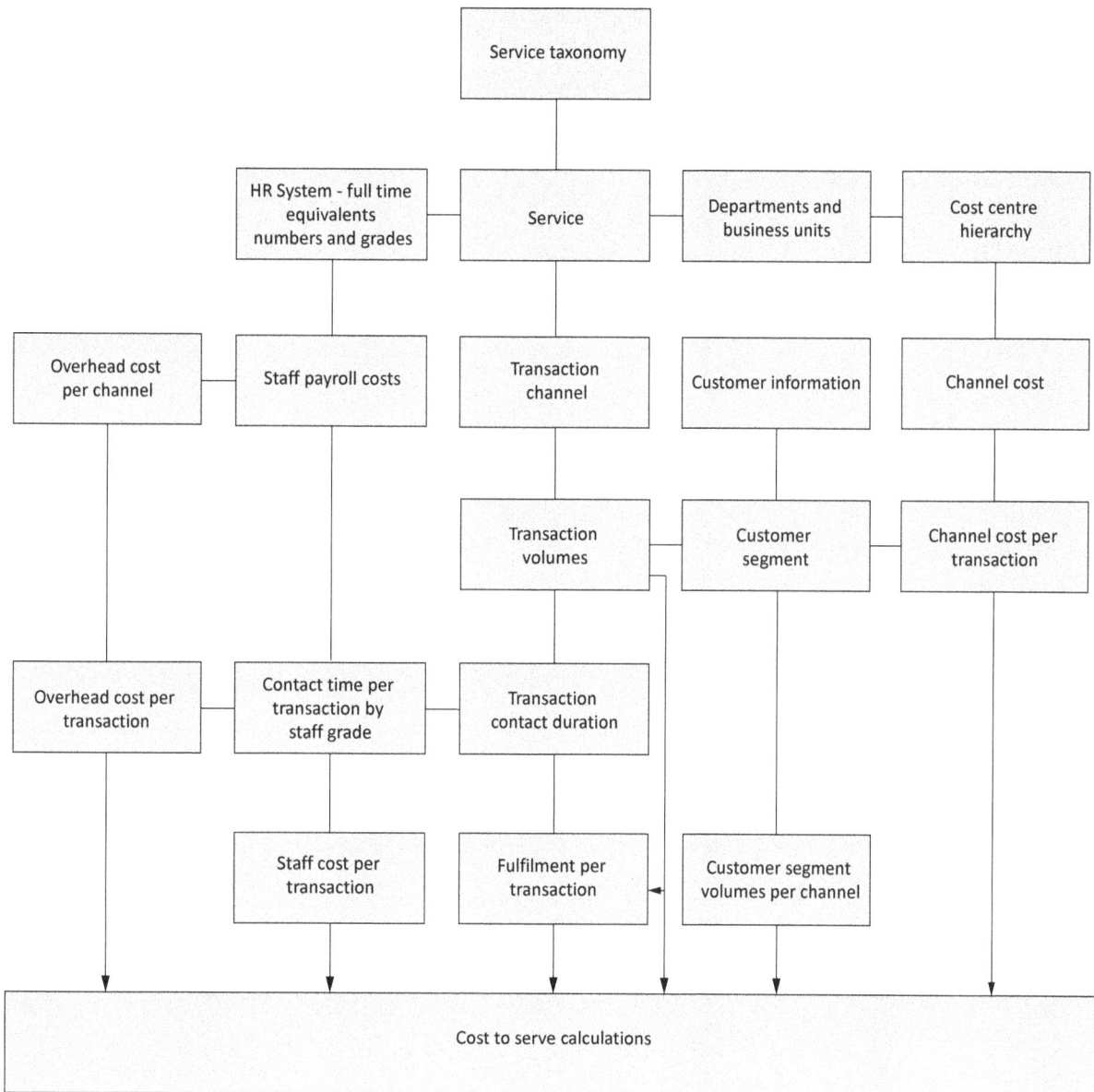

```
                              ┌──────────────────┐
                              │ Service taxonomy │
                              └──────────────────┘

┌────────────────┐   ┌──────────┐   ┌──────────────┐   ┌──────────────┐
│ HR System -    │   │          │   │ Departments  │   │ Cost centre  │
│ full time      │───│ Service  │───│ and business │───│ hierarchy    │
│ equivalents    │   │          │   │ units        │   │              │
│ numbers and    │   │          │   │              │   │              │
│ grades         │   │          │   │              │   │              │
└────────────────┘   └──────────┘   └──────────────┘   └──────────────┘

┌─────────────┐ ┌──────────────┐ ┌────────────┐ ┌──────────────┐ ┌────────────┐
│ Overhead    │ │ Staff        │ │ Transaction│ │ Customer     │ │ Channel    │
│ cost per    │─│ payroll      │ │ channel    │ │ information  │ │ cost       │
│ channel     │ │ costs        │ │            │ │              │ │            │
└─────────────┘ └──────────────┘ └────────────┘ └──────────────┘ └────────────┘

                 ┌──────────────┐ ┌────────────┐ ┌──────────────┐
                 │ Transaction  │ │ Customer   │ │ Channel cost │
                 │ volumes      │ │ segment    │ │ per          │
                 │              │ │            │ │ transaction  │
                 └──────────────┘ └────────────┘ └──────────────┘

┌─────────────┐ ┌──────────────┐ ┌────────────┐
│ Overhead    │ │ Contact time │ │ Transaction│
│ cost per    │─│ per          │─│ contact    │
│ transaction │ │ transaction  │ │ duration   │
│             │ │ by staff     │ │            │
│             │ │ grade        │ │            │
└─────────────┘ └──────────────┘ └────────────┘

                 ┌──────────────┐ ┌────────────┐ ┌──────────────┐
                 │ Staff cost   │ │ Fulfilment │ │ Customer     │
                 │ per          │ │ per        │ │ segment      │
                 │ transaction  │ │ transaction│ │ volumes per  │
                 │              │ │            │ │ channel      │
                 └──────────────┘ └────────────┘ └──────────────┘

┌────────────────────────────────────────────────────────────────────┐
│                      Cost to serve calculations                     │
└────────────────────────────────────────────────────────────────────┘
```

4.1.7 Metadata

Metadata is data that provides information about other data. It plays a crucial role in ensuring that the exercise is transparent and repeatable. AI algorithms often rely on metadata to understand, process, and interpret information effectively. Metadata in machine learning is used for training AI models. Metadata is also fundamental for indexing and retrieving specific information efficiently. In the future some or all your cost to serve data could be retrieved by AI.

4.1.8 Support and training

Providing coaching or establishing a coaching champion network for business units needing assistance with data collection and process time estimation can be beneficial. Consider conducting workshops with relevant stakeholders to facilitate information gathering across organisational silos. Additionally, offering training or creating a community of practice can help develop and support staff in utilising the new capability after the project concludes.

5.0 Suggested project workstreams

A cost to serve project will require the collection of data from various parts of the organisation. The project has been divided into seven workstreams:

1. Cost centre mapping
2. Customer transactions
3. Staffing and costs
4. Staff utilisation
5. Access channels
6. Customer segmentation
7. Data management

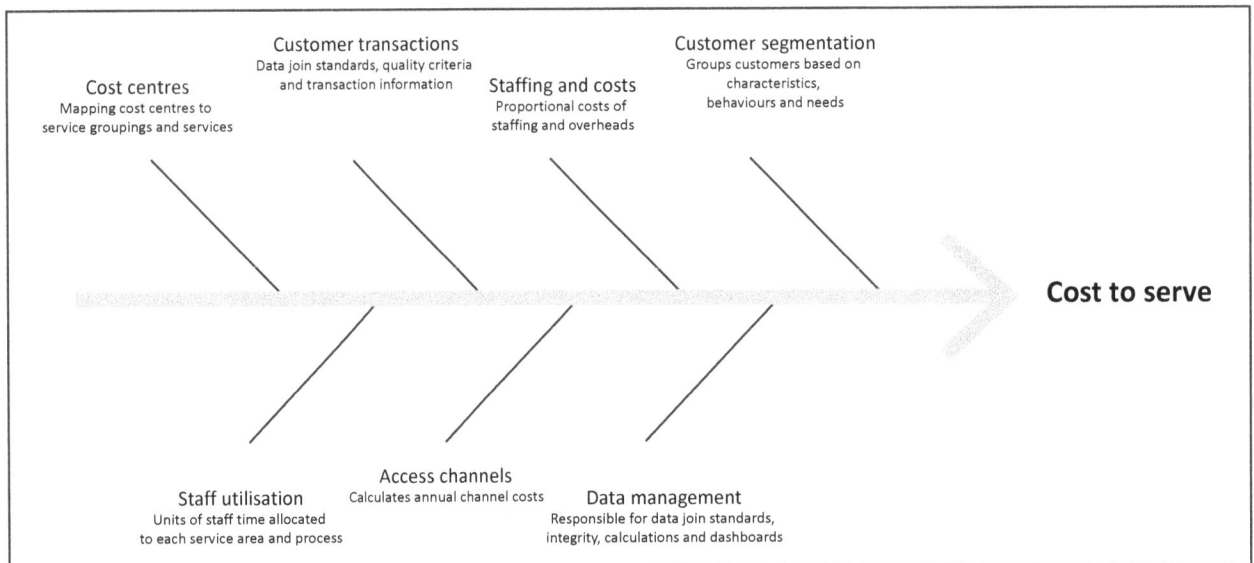

The rationales for the workstreams are as follows:

1. **Cost centre mapping:** This workstream focuses on extracting cost data from financial systems, specifically connecting costs from the general ledger to services, access channels, and resources.

2. **Customer transactions:** A service is characterised as the offering and the specific ways customers interact with the offering. The aim is to identify the transactions within the defined scope or establish standards for their identification. When services are identified, transaction data covering a specified period should be obtained. The

next step is to estimate staff contact time – the average time (in minutes) it takes a member of staff to service each request type. The comprehensive calculation might include front-office time, plus back-office time, and where applicable the time or cost of fulfilment. Summary data is limiting, therefore this workstream should aim to work with and extract summaries from individual transaction records.

3. **Staffing and costs:** This workstream aims to establish organisational standards for calculating annual productive minutes for full-time equivalent staff, and for apportioning direct and indirect costs per head. Additionally, it seeks to identify the cost of staff time per grade, per minute. The total cost per employee per head is calculated by combining direct and indirect costs per head and dividing this by annual productive minutes per head.

4. **Staff utilisation:** This workstream is responsible for collating staff utilisation percentages and calculating the cost of delivering each service transaction, based on average processing times and staff cost per minute. This is especially useful where staff work on more than one service, in more than one service area, or where the organisation wants to look at the cost of delivering distinct aspects of a service. Collating assumed utilisation adds valuable context to the staff utilisation figures that will automatically come out of the cost to serve calculation.

5. **Access channels:** An access channel refers to the delivery medium or platform through which individuals, organisations, or entities can obtain or gain access to a service, information, or resource. It serves as a pathway or means of communication, interaction, or connection between the service provider and the customer. Access channels can be physical, virtual, digital, or distribution. Because they are diverse, they have different cost bases. The full cost of delivering a service will therefore differ,

depending on the channels available and/or the channel a customer chooses to use. While the back office is not traditionally considered an access channel, it should be treated as one for the purpose of the calculation. This approach supports the incorporation of fixed and variable metrics, enabling you to cost the end-to-end service. By including back-office processing in the analysis, you can explore opportunities for a more comprehensive understanding and evaluation of costs associated with the entire process.

6. **Customer segmentation:** This entails outlining your segmentation aims and incorporating actionable customer segmentation objectives into the list of outcomes. To include this, you should collect permissible customer data along with each transaction record, map the customer identifiers to existing segmentation information and/or include segmentation modelling data, and let your segmentation professional do the rest.

7. **Data management:** While the cost to serve calculation is straightforward, it is crucial to mitigate the risk of not being able to justify or obtain the same results from repeating a calculation. To uphold quality assurance, it is recommended to designate a suitable individual or team responsible for capturing assumptions, recording data cleansing and data matching rules, recording stakeholder consultations, assumptions, and caveats, and establishing a process for assigning data quality rankings and quality signoffs. This workstream will also manage the presentation of data, ranging from being the custodian of the data repository to being responsible for the development of a wider data exploration and usage. This ensures that the initial repository data serves as a baseline against which to measure future inputs.

Workstream leads will expect to receive the following artefacts from you:

1. The organisational objectives in relation to the project

2. The project scope

3. This suggested workstream chapter for context

4. The depth of the analysis required

5. Guidance on data quality standards recording

6. The format for and guidance on documenting the quality sign off process

7. The format for collating an audit trail of what was done, by whom, processes, working assumptions, consultation processes, caveats, and work arounds

Associated deliverables for each workstream

Cost centre mapping

- Business units
- Services hierarchies
- Resource hierarchies
- Access channels

Customer interactions

- Front- and back-office transactions
- Service identifiers
- Transaction volumes
- Transaction durations (minutes)
- Process/data flow maps
- Variable processing costs
- Customer profiles with each transaction record
- Average fulfilment cost per transaction per annum (e.g. the cost of goods, packaging, transportation, storage, equipment, maintenance, staff, equipment, etc.)
- Customer fulfilment and outsourced contracts

Access channels

- Fixed annual channel costs
- Variable processing costs

Staffing and costs

- FTEs per service area
- Average annual productive minutes
- Direct staff cost per service/service area
- Indirect staff costs per service area
- Average annual salary per FTE per service area
- On costs per head
- Staff cost per minute

Staff utilisation

- Average annual staff numbers, by service and pay scale
- Estimated staff utilisation by service or service group
- Opportunity costs of alternative staffing configurations

Customer segmentation

- Actionable segmentation analysis

Data management

- Data quality, formatting and matching and consistency
- Data repository
- Cost to serve calculations
- Drillable dashboards
- Reporting
- KPIs

Do not forget the Workshops

Analysing the cost to serve demands a comprehensive grasp of processes, hand-offs, systems, and challenges. Involving a diverse group of stakeholders promotes a more expansive view of intricacies. Collaboration aids in aligning thoughts towards shared objectives and applying a holistic approach to possible solutions cultivates relationships among various organisational units, nurturing an atmosphere conducive to continuous creativity and innovation.

5.1 Cost centre mapping workstream

Mapping general ledger codes to services

Aligning general ledger codes with departments, services, and staff resources is essential for the accurate cost attribution of services.

Objective

The purpose of the project is to identify the average cost for delivering each service within the scope of the exercise.

The purpose of this workstream is to map cost centres from the general ledger to departments, services, and resources.

Main deliverables

1. Department and business unit cost data, from a mapping of cost centre IDs to departments and business units (must have)

2. Service and/or service group cost data, from a mapping of cost centre IDs to service IDs or service groups (should have)

3. Resource costs per service data, from a mapping of cost centre IDs to resource hierarchies and related overheads (should have)

4. Access channel cost data, from a mapping of cost centre IDs to access channels (must have)

5. Documentation of the process and the assumptions made sufficiently detailed to ensure the exercise is repeatable (must have)

Prerequisites

From the project manager you will receive

1. The project scope

2. The depth of the analysis required

3. The organisational objectives in relation to this project

4. An overview of all the workstreams

5. Agreed budget year that the base data should represent

6. Data quality standards recording guidance

7. Services within scope from the customer transactions workstream

8. Staff grades and utilisation percentages against the services within scope from the customer transactions workstream

9. Data collection standards documentation with a high-level data map

Your organisation is unique, you should therefore do the mapping your way. As a general guide, the following outlines the steps commonly used.

Use accounting software: Numerous accounting software solutions provide functionalities for aligning general ledger codes with departments and services. Take advantage of existing tools and utilise pre-existing mappings where their accuracy is assured.

Streamlined requirements for the cost centre mapping workstream

Use your understanding of the general ledger codes to:

- **Identify departments and services:** List all the departments and services within scope, include departmental expenditure, payroll, agency, and other staffing costs.

- **Create a mapping table:** List each general ledger code and its corresponding department or service. This table will serve as a reference point for cost allocations.

- **Allocate costs** to the appropriate departments or services based on the mapping.

- **Review and update:** Periodically review and update your mapping table. This is crucial as organisational changes, new services, or modified expense categories may require adjustments.

- **Maintain documentation:** Record the mapping process, decisions, collaborations, and assumptions. Documenting the process is essential for auditing, financial reporting, repeatability, and transparency.

That is it! However, as is common with most endeavours, there are additional layers of complexity. When utilising the simplified requirements, it is recommended to set the data quality ranking to three stars. This is because the calculation relies on evidence, but the evidence lacks nuance to consider all factors comprehensively. For a more nuanced evaluation, refer to the comprehensive requirements below as a guide, and if you adopt all or parts of it, adjust the data quality ranking score accordingly.

Comprehensive requirements for the cost centre workstream

Add the following considerations to the streamlined requirements above:

- *Analyse expense categories:* Review the general ledger codes, specifically the expense accounts. These are accounts that most often need to be mapped to departments and services. Examples include office supplies, salaries, utilities, and travel expenses, which may need to be apportioned.

- *Collaborate with stakeholders:* To gain a better understanding of the costs related to business units, departments, and services, work collaboratively with relevant stakeholders. Test assumptions, verify mappings, and maintain a record of the gathered information. Collaboration with stakeholders is particularly valuable in cases where staff are utilised in more than one service area.

- *Check big ticket items:* Where cost centre expense codes on your general ledger lack clarity, it may be necessary to probe further. Additionally, auditing invoices over a specific threshold can be used to allocate or apportion expenses accurately to the respective service(s).

Outline data requirements

The minimum requirement for shallow and broad and shallow/narrow implementations is a mapping between the cost centre hierarchy, business units and the staff that the business units employ. To allocate cost to individual services, the mapping will need to extend beyond business units to the individual services that the business units deliver, and the full-time equivalent staff allocated to deliver each service.

Where cost centre expense codes on your general ledger lack clarity, it may be necessary to probe further. Include the proportional cost of any supply chains, preferably listed under distinct headings to enhance readability and facilitate future analysis. Additionally, auditing invoices over a specific threshold is often needed to allocate and apportion them accurately. This will ensure that costs are correctly mapped to the right business units/services. Collaboration with stakeholders is particularly valuable in cases where staff are utilised in more than one service area.

Suggested data map for cost centre workstream

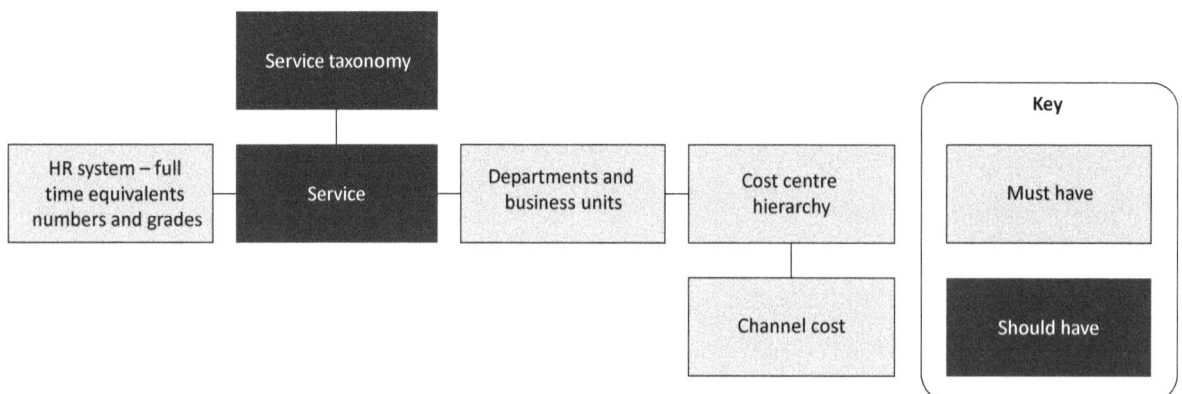

38

5.2 Customer transactions workstream

Identify service names and groupings

The objective of this workstream is to collate the list of services your organisation offers and link them to transaction metrics. This may be a simple exercise where you use what is already there. However, you may need to break a service down further where the offering results in more than one deliverable or uses different resources depending on the desired outcome. Use an agreed standard for identifying service components. An example of a standard is GS1, a barcode system used in the retail industry for sharing information about products, locations and assets. Another example is the international network of food data systems used for describing foods to facilitate international exchange. A service list can be referred to as a taxonomy. A taxonomy of services is a systematic classification or hierarchical arrangement of assorted services based on their characteristics, attributes, or functions. It is a structured framework that helps to organise services into distinct and meaningful groups, allowing for easier management, analysis, and understanding. It is like creating a 'family tree' of services, where you can see how different services are related, grouped, or categorised. A taxonomy is therefore a valuable tool for structuring services, to support clarity of understanding for internal and external stakeholders. It is also scalable.

Objective

The purpose of the project is to identify the average cost for delivering each service within the scope of the exercise.

The purpose of this workstream is to use existing standard descriptions or produce a list or taxonomy of services within scope and collect service transaction metrics against it. The results will serve as the foundation for measuring the cost to serve.

Main deliverables

1. A taxonomy of agreed services or service groups (must have)

2. Mapping between front and back-office processing (should have)

3. Transaction records from which volumes can be derived, against each service delivered via the access channels within scope (must have)

4. Transaction records against which volumes can be derived, against each sub-service delivered via the access channels within scope (should have)

5. Transaction records to include actual or estimated contract durations (must have)

6. Transaction records to include dates and times (should have)

7. Maps of the systems utilised to deliver each service (should have)

8. Identification of variable costs linked to each service (should have)

9. Direct cost of fulfilling each transaction – this might include printing, posting, packaging, or the cost of a physical thing being delivered, where delivery is included in the cost (should have)

10. Identification of the purpose and costs of outsourced contracts linked to service provision

11. Transaction records to include permissible customer information for segmentation purposes (could have)

12. Documentation of the process, assumptions, consultations, calculations, data matching algorithms, caveats, data quality ratings and quality sign off documentation (must have)

Prerequisites

From the project manager you will receive:

a. The project scope

b. The depth of the analysis required

c. An overview of all the workstreams

d. The organisational objectives in relation to this project

e. Data quality standards recording guidance

Decide on the quality criteria for your organisation

If you have a developed catalogue of services (taxonomy) in place for each access channel, use it to collate service metrics against. For online services, include the URLs. If your catalogue of services is not robust, see the guidance below. You might find the following quality criteria with responsibilities useful.

#	Quality criteria	Responsibility
1.	Relevance: Ensure that the taxonomy accurately represents the services offered and their relationships and reflects business objectives and customer needs	This workstream's lead
2.	Consistency: Maintain uniform terminology and classification rules throughout the taxonomy to avoid confusion and ambiguity	This workstream's lead
3.	Clarity: Make the taxonomy easy to understand for both internal and external stakeholders, using plain language and clear definitions	This workstream's lead
4.	Hierarchy: Create a logical hierarchical structure that allows for nested categories and subcategories representing the relationships between services	This workstream's lead
5.	Completeness: Ensure that the taxonomy includes all relevant services and that no critical services are omitted from the classification	Based on scope
6.	Flexibility: Design the taxonomy to be adaptable and accommodating of changes as new services are introduced or existing ones are modified	This workstream's lead
7.	Accuracy: Ensure that each service is categorised accurately and that there are no misclassifications or duplications	Service Managers
8.	User-centricity: Prioritise the taxonomy's usability for customers or end-users, making it easy for them to find the services they need	User experience design
9.	Regulatory compliance: Ensure that the taxonomy accounts for any industry-specific regulations or compliance requirements, allowing for accurate reporting and auditing	Service managers
10.	Scalability: Design the taxonomy with scalability in mind, allowing for the addition of new services without disrupting the existing structure	Service managers
11.	Cross-referencing: Implement cross-referencing mechanisms to link related services or categories, enhancing the ability to explore interconnected services	Service managers
12.	Documentation: Maintain comprehensive documentation for the taxonomy, including definitions, classification rules, and any changes or updates over time	This workstream's lead
13.	Feedback mechanisms: Established for collecting feedback from stakeholders to continuously improve the taxonomy's effectiveness and accuracy	Project manager
14.	Data consistency: Ensure that data collected and reported using the taxonomy is consistent and standardised, allowing for accurate analysis and reporting	Data Lead
15.	Governance: Implement governance processes to oversee and maintain the taxonomy's quality, including periodic reviews and updates	Project Manager
16.	Benchmarking: Take the future ability to benchmark against industry standards into account during the design	This workstream's lead

Examples of developed service taxonomies can be found at www.data.gov.uk. – Local Government Service List

Guidance for developing a taxonomy or for checking that an existing taxonomy is fit for purpose

Use the list you have. However, if some areas are not clear, you may need to do some work to define services so they are distinctly identifiable. Organise your services into hierarchical groups as they are structured and delivered by the organisation. For areas where deeper analysis is required, identify individual transaction types.

Services offered to customers are usually grouped, one way of thinking of a service grouping is like a tree with branches representing several types of service and leaves representing specific offerings. For an educational institution this might be a faculty which offers accredited courses, and those courses consist of subjects. There would be more than one faculty, more than one course, and many subjects. A subject could be relevant to more than one course. Examples of goods and services that can be repeated are receiving payment, authenticating that the customer is who they say they are, and making a complaint.

- Level 1 – Tree   Faculty
- Level 2 – Branch   Course
- Level 3 – Leaf   Subject

For an insurance company:

- Level 1 – Tree   Car insurance
- Level 2 – Branch   Group
- Level 3 – Leaf   Policy type

For a local authority, that might mean a department such as environment, where:

- Level 1 – Tree   Environment
- Level 2 – Branch   Rubbish and recycling
- Level 3 – Leaf   Missed bin collections

> This level will differentiate costs by service group

> This level will differentiate costs by service

Level 1 ID	Level 1 Name	Level 2 ID	Level 2 Name	Level 3 ID	Level 3 Name
30	Environment	38	Waste Management	528	Bulky household waste collection
30	Environment	38	Waste Management	530	Garden waste
30	Environment	38	Waste Management	854	Assisted collection
30	Environment	38	Waste Management	534	Recycling sites
30	Environment	38	Waste Management	524	Household waste collection

> This level will differentiate costs by department

5.2.1 Collect service data

Identify your service data and capture the hierarchical relationships between departments, natural groupings, and service names. This will be useful for reporting later. There may be a need at this stage to capture service attributes. For example, a service like food premises licencing can have many attributes – you could apply, appeal a decision, update, pay, request a status update, and complain. Although all these requests relate to the same service, they are different and where possible you should attempt to capture these differences. For example, if 30% of the enquiries relate to requesting a service update to check on the status of an existing application, then there is something that you could do to improve the customer experience and reduce the cost to serve. Tackling failure demand information requests may be as simple as managing expectations at the start of the process and/or reducing processing wait times and/or building in the provision of self-service or automatic updates. Having identified the services delivered, you now need to collate data against each leaf level service.

Identify service attributes/interactions: One way of identifying service attributes is to use a list of activities to identify what they are for each service. Examples of service attributes include: enquiring, applying, reporting, cancelling, paying, booking, responding, complaining, registering, updating, challenging, appealing, checking the status, and providing information. If it is not practical to break every service down in this way, consider targeting high-volume and problematic services for this treatment.

Web analytics

For online services, web analytics provides insights into customer behaviour at crucial points during the customer journey. These behavioural insights contribute significantly to understanding the customer experience and capturing the voice of the customer. They, along with app analytics, form an integral part of the cost to serve data pool, enabling identification of where customers abandon their journey, feedback on their experience, or seek alternative means of contact, and the savings that could ensue if the customer experience is improved. Integrating web and app analytics with operational data creates a comprehensive view for multichannel cost to serve analysis, allowing for a more detailed understanding of customer behaviour, motivations, and needs.

Because web and app analytics dashboards offer varied content and configuration choices, providing specific example templates is not feasible here. However, the focus should encompass the accessed service, as this linkage is crucial for connecting customer contacts across various channels. Attributes such as uniform resource locator (URL), service identifiers (department, business unit, service, and service interaction), goal completion, sessions, users, bounce rates, average customer time to convert, use of chatbots and session durations, among others, will also be valuable for analysis.

Telephone and walk-in centres summary transaction record example

The process of collecting, analysing, and interpreting data related to telephone contact between customers and the call centre agents involves monitoring volumes, durations, first call resolutions, and costs. An example of a telephone and face-to-face contact template is provided below.

Level 1 Name	Level 2	Level 3	Level 4	Annual or annualised transaction volumes	Transaction date and time	Transaction durations	Wrap-up durations	Calls resolved on first contact
Environment	Licences	Food registration	Apply	99,999	dd/mm/yy 00:00:00	hh/mm/ss	hh/mm/ss	99,999
Environment	Licences	Food registration	Pay	99,999	dd/mm/yy 00:00:00	hh/mm/ss	hh/mm/ss	99,999
Environment	Licences	Food registration	Appeal	99,999	dd/mm/yy 00:00:00	hh/mm/ss	hh/mm/ss	99,999
Environment	Licences	Food registration	Status enquiry	99,999	dd/mm/yy 00:00:00	hh/mm/ss	hh/mm/ss	99,999

Systemic data mapping

Having identified the services in scope you may find it useful to develop simple high-level decision trees to identify the systems that hold data related to each transaction type, as this builds the knowledge for costing the processing of each stage.

Level 1 Name	Level 2 Name	Level 3 Name	Level 3 Attribute	System 1 CRM	System 2 Apply	System 3 Pay	System 4 Complain	Back office
Environment	Licences	Food registration	Apply	Yes	Yes	Yes		Yes
Environment	Licences	Food registration	Complain	Yes			Yes	
Environment	Licences	Food registration	Appeal	Yes				Yes
Environment	Licences	Food registration	Status enquiry	Yes				Yes

Supply chain and fulfilment cost

Supply chain costs relate to the price of procuring raw materials for transformation into goods or services. Supply chain costs are captured in the cost centre mapping workstream. Fulfilment costs relates to any additional costs involved in completing the service request if fulfilment is not outsourced. It is worth knowing the actual cost, even if this is covered by the customer. Fulfilment includes the cost of configuration, customisations, as well as expenses related to delivery, attendance, installation, equipment/ machine hours, or the cost of handing the service request to a third party for completion.

Where service fulfilment is outsourced, there may be a stated cost for each service type within the contract. Where the contract price is fixed, divide the annual value of the contract by the number of annual transactions to arrive at the cost to serve per transaction.

Where the costs involve delivery of a service at the customer's location, and where there is not an existing method for calculating the cost, consider costs related to parts, equipment, transportation, packing materials, labour, and other indirect expenses.

Fulfilment costs per transaction

For each service:

- Sum up the average annual costs associated with each component (labour, parts, equipment, transportation, etc.) and divide the sum by the number of transactions to obtain the average cost of fulfilling that type of service request

- Include overhead costs

Data collection suggestions

1. Build the transaction record – a transaction record should contain as much information as possible

2. Include back-office processing durations where required or appropriate

3. Include front and back-office use of systems

4. Include fulfilment information where relevant

5. Include the fixed and variable systems and resources used to deliver the process

6. Create data and systems maps to support discussions

Suggested data map for customer transactions workstream

When fulfilment costs are an integral part of the service offering, the actual cost of fulfilment should be separately identified.

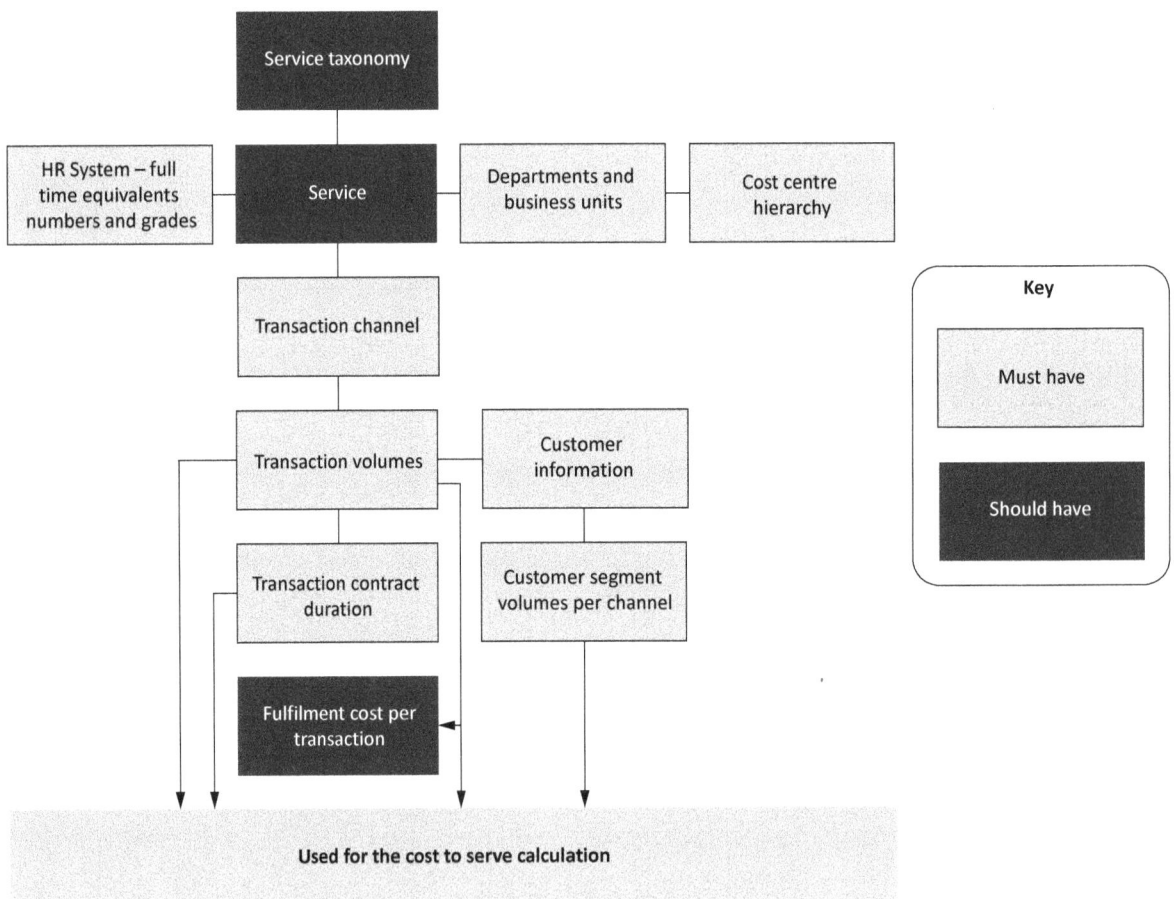

```
                    ┌──────────────────┐
                    │ Service taxonomy │
                    └──────────────────┘
                             │
┌──────────────┐    ┌────────────┐    ┌──────────────┐    ┌──────────────┐
│ HR System –  │    │            │    │ Departments  │    │ Cost centre  │
│ full time    │────│  Service   │────│ and business │────│ hierarchy    │
│ equivalents  │    │            │    │ units        │    │              │
│ numbers and  │    └────────────┘    └──────────────┘    └──────────────┘
│ grades       │
└──────────────┘
                             │
                    ┌──────────────────┐
                    │ Transaction      │
                    │ channel          │
                    └──────────────────┘
                             │
                    ┌──────────────┐    ┌──────────────┐
                    │ Transaction  │────│ Customer     │
                    │ volumes      │    │ information  │
                    └──────────────┘    └──────────────┘
                             │                  │
                    ┌──────────────┐    ┌──────────────────┐
                    │ Transaction  │    │ Customer segment │
                    │ contract     │    │ volumes per      │
                    │ duration     │    │ channel          │
                    └──────────────┘    └──────────────────┘
                             │
                    ┌──────────────────┐
                    │ Fulfilment cost  │
                    │ per transaction  │
                    └──────────────────┘

      Used for the cost to serve calculation
```

Key

| Must have |
| Should have |

Customer transaction summary

The transaction data required for the calculation includes transaction volumes for each access channel and service, average transaction durations for each access channel and service, and average wrap up and/or processing times.

Calculation	Description	Data	Suggested data source	Must have/should have	Formula reference
Annual transaction volumes for each service and access channel	Records containing rows of individual transactions for each service over a determined period	Transaction records	• Line of business systems • Telephone switch data • CRM • Payment systems	Must have	Annual channel transactions
Average transaction contact minutes	The average time spent by staff with the customer in the channel	Usually included with telephone switch data, case records, IVR and/or CRM	• Telephone switch data • Queue management systems • Live chat • Manual tick sheets	Must have	Average transaction minutes
Average wrap up time per contact	The average time that an agent spends completing various tasks after the conclusion of a call or interaction with a customer	The average time after a case before the agent is available to work on the next case	• Telephone switch data • Queue management systems • Staff interviews • Manual tick sheets	Must have	Average transaction minutes
Annual back-office transactions	The annual number of transactions passed to the back office for processing	Transaction volumes data	• Line of business systems • CRM	Should have	Annual back-office transactions
Average back-office processing minutes	The average time that staff spend completing various tasks related to a service request	The average processing time for each service request or case	• Workshops • Tick sheet exercise over a week or two • Staff/ stakeholder interviews	Should have	Average back-office processing time
Average fulfilment cost per transaction	Expenses involved in getting a physical product or service to the customer	• Service level agreement • Contact transaction volumes divided by annual costs.	• Annual fulfilment contract value • Annual transactions	Must have	Fulfilment cost per transaction

Customer support costs Failure demand refers to customer requests or enquiries that arise because of a failure in delivering a product or service to the customer's satisfaction. It is demand that occurs when there is a breakdown in the normal functioning of a system or process, leading customers to seek additional assistance, corrections, or redress. Customer support costs falling into this category can be measured separately as a failure demand overhead, because technically the costs are unnecessary. If this approach is taken, it is advisable to share the results with the relevant service leads and experts to verify that the findings, and any assumptions made, reflect their understanding of how the service is delivered.

Do not forget to record and outline your assumptions and approach to ensure that the process is auditable and repeatable.

5.3 Staffing and costs workstream

The purpose of the project is to identify the average cost for delivering each service within the scope of the exercise.

This workstream is divided into two parts:

1. Calculating and costing full-time equivalents (FTEs) for each service

2. Calculating and apportioning overheads to each FTE

5.31 Calculating and costing full-time equivalents

The purpose of this workstream is to calculate annual FTE minutes available to deliver services and FTE costs per minute.

Requirements

The outputs from the customer interactions workstream, mapped to cost centres, which will provide a list of services in scope for each channel and the assumed average annual staff time spent on delivering each service.

Prerequisites

From the project manager you will receive:

1. The project scope

2. The depth of the analysis required

3. The organisational objectives in relation to this project

4. An overview of all the workstreams

5. Outputs from the customer interactions workstream

6. Data quality standards recording guidance

7. Formats for documenting the process and quality sign off requirements

Deliverables

1. Number of FTE staff per service (must have)

2. Estimated annual staff time by pay band spent on delivering each service, for each access channel (should have) OR

3. Estimated annual staff time based on proportional business unit staffing expenses for each service, by access channel (must have)

4. Assumptions and quality sign off for this workstream (must have)

5. Documentation outlining the process – this might include assumptions, work arounds, stakeholder consultations, calculations, data matching algorithms, caveats, data quality ratings and quality sign off documentation (must have)

Guidance

Your organisation is likely to have a method for calculating FTE staff numbers and you should use it if it serves the purpose. The following method of calculating FTE staff would receive a five-star data quality rating. Rate your method accordingly.

1. Hours of work: Determine the standard hours of work per week for full-time, part-time, and casual employees.

2. Leave entitlements: Factor in distinct types of leave entitlements such as annual leave, sick leave, and long service leave.

3. Public holidays: Consider the number of public holidays in a year and whether employees are entitled to paid leave on those days.

4. Overtime: Consider the extent to which employees work overtime and the overtime rates payable.

5. Part-time and casual staff: Convert the hours worked by part-time and casual employees to FTE equivalents.

6. Seasonal variations: Consider any seasonal variations in staffing requirements and adjust FTE staff numbers accordingly.

7. Management cost allocation: Allocate tiered management time and associated costs to respective services. Record this information in distinct columns, as a component of indirect costs to enhance transparency and facilitate effective analysis.

Full-time equivalent (FTE) is a term used in staffing to describe the number of hours worked by an employee. One FTE represents one full-time staff member. FTE is used to measure a part-time employee's working hours relative to a full-time employee, considering the number of hours that a part-time employee works as a proportion of a full-time employee's hours. The calculation of staffing costs requires the conversion of part-time staff into FTEs. FTE calculations are commonly used for budgeting purposes to determine the total cost of labour for a specific project or department. It is especially useful for resource planning, budgeting, performance measurement, and workforce optimisation. It is also an essential prerequisite for cost to serve.

With zero-hours contracts and contractors you need only take contracted time into account. Employees' annual productive minutes refer to the total amount of time that an employee spends actively engaged in work-related tasks over the course of a year. This includes time spent on direct work activities – such as meeting with clients, producing reports, or completing assignments – as well as indirect work activities – such as attending training sessions, staff meetings, etc.

Calculating annual productive minutes typically involves subtracting time spent on non-productive activities (such as vacations, sick leave, and other forms of leave entitlements) from the total number of minutes in a year (525,600). For example, if an employee takes 20 days of vacation leave and 10 days of sick leave in a year, the total non-productive time would be 30 days, or 4,320 minutes. Therefore, the total annual productive minutes for this employee would be 521,280 (525,600 minus 4,320). Consider excluding outliers and using organisation-wide estimates as a basis for your FTE calculations.

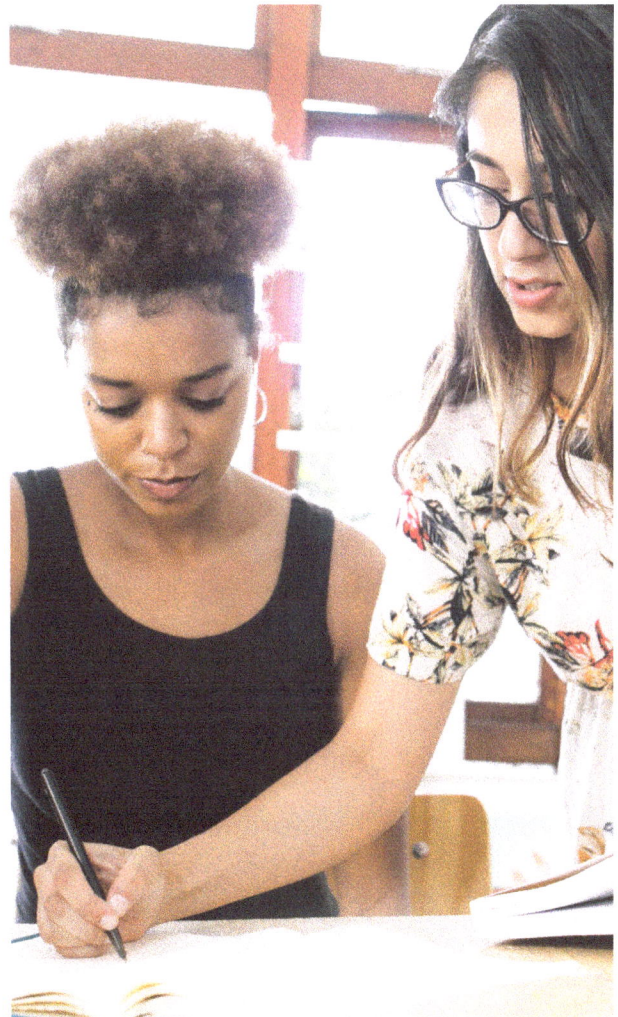

Suggested data map for staffing and cost workstreams

A mapping from the cost centre hierarchy to departments/business units, the staff that work within them, and how much they are paid is required.

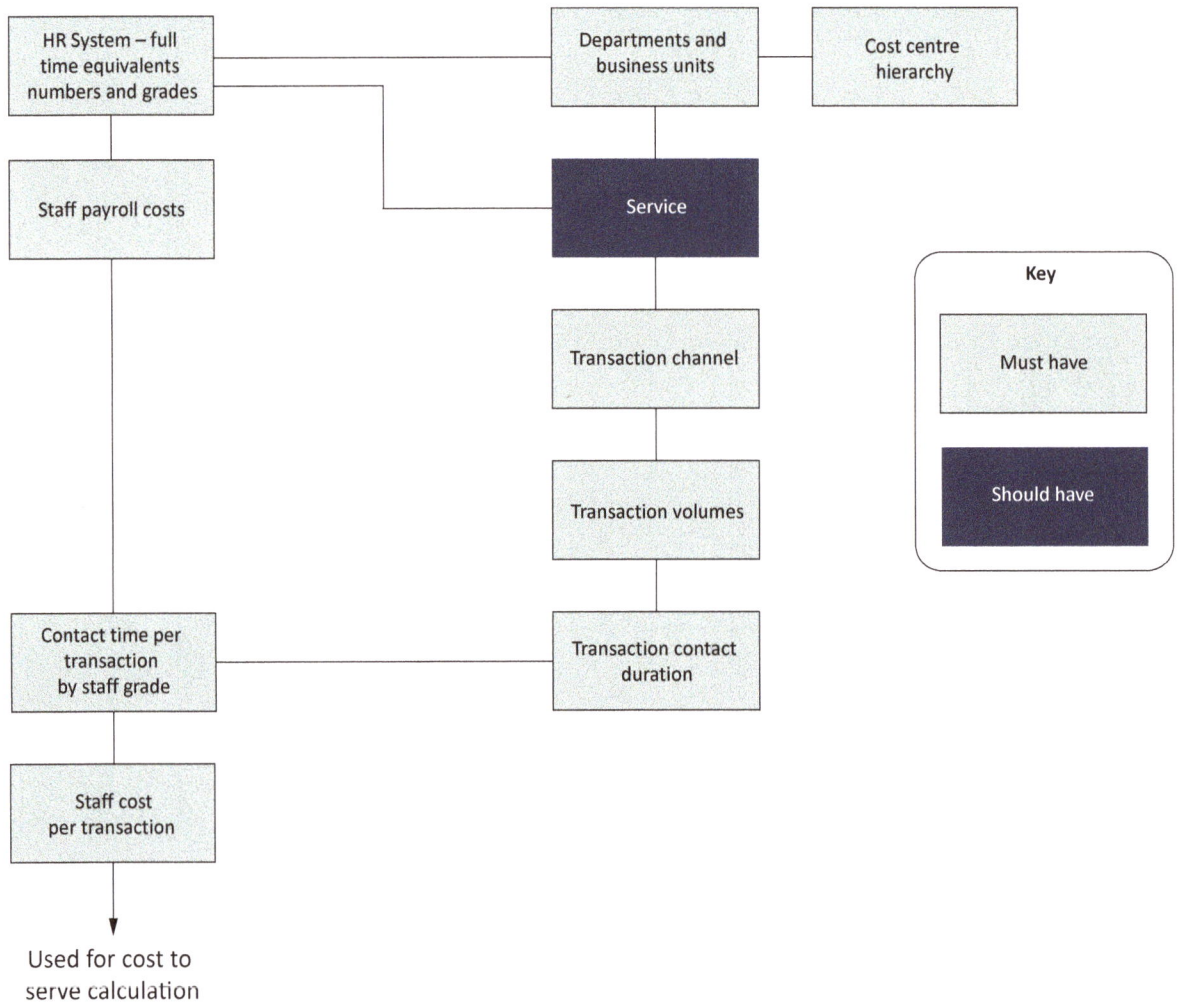

Full-time equivalent calculation

The purpose of this exercise is to arrive at the annual productive minutes available to each service area using a standard FTE formula. Unless there is good reason, the assumptions about holidays, time off, training, etc. should be applied across the organisation.

Full-time equivalent (FTE) calculation example

A food premises licensing department has four employees, two of them work full time while the other two work part time. Of the part-time workers, one employee works 20 hours per week and the other works 30 hours per week. The company's standard full-time work week is 40 hours. The total hours worked by all four employees is therefore 130 hours per week. However, to arrive at the number of productive minutes, the calculation needs to take time off into account. To do this we must calculate the annual minutes for all employees.

Linking the cost to serve with the ability to measure staff productive minutes per business unit and productivity by staff pay spine point provides a comprehensive approach to evaluating operational efficiency and financial performance. By tracking the productive minutes of staff within each business unit, organisations can gain insights into how effectively time is being utilised to meet service demands. This granular data, when aligned with the pay spine points, enables a precise assessment of productivity relative to employee compensation levels. Consequently, businesses can identify make informed decisions on resource allocation and cost management. This integrated measurement framework not only highlights areas where efficiency can be improved but also helps in optimising staffing costs and enhancing overall service delivery.

Estimated productive staff minutes available per annum	E12345	E23456	E34567	E45678	Total
Employee number	E12345	E23456	E34567	E45678	
Employee salary spine point	18	19	19	20	
Full time equivalence (FTE)	1	0.75	0.5	1	3.25
Working week hours[1]	40	30	20	40	130
Average number of hours per day	8	6	4	8	26
Working days available per year (assuming a five-day week)	260	260	260	260	1040
Estimated training days per year	5	5	5	5	20
Estimated sick days per year	5	4	3	5	17
Annual leave days	25	18.75	12.5	26	82.25
Public holidays	8	8	8	8	32
Non-working days / year (sum of (training+sick+leave+public holidays))	43	36	29	44	151
Actual working days / year (available days minus non-working days)	217	224	232	216	889
Non-working hrs. / year (non-working days*calculated hrs. / day)	344	215	114	352	1,025
Available working hrs / year (wk. hrs.*wk./year (52) – non-working hrs.)	1,736	1,346	926	1,728	5,736
Available minutes / year (available hrs. / annum *minutes /hr. (60))	104,160	80,730	55,560	103,680	344,130
Annual productive minutes	104,160	80,730	55,560	103,680	344,130

[1] Standard working hours = 40.

Average annual productive minutes available to the business unit = 344,130

Mapping services to FTE data

The outputs from this workstream are FTE numbers together with a calculation of average annual productive minutes mapped to each service or service area.

Quality sign-off

The quality sign-off of the approach and assumptions will require staffing numbers validation with service managers.

5.32 Calculating and apportioning overheads to each FTE

Objective

The purpose of the project is to identify the average cost for delivering each service within the scope of the exercise.

The purpose of this workstream is to apportion organisational overheads to services, to estimate the staff cost for delivering the services within scope.

Prerequisites

From the project manager you will receive:

1. The project scope
2. The depth of the analysis required
3. The organisational objectives in relation to this project
4. Data quality standards guidance
5. An overview of all the workstreams
6. Estimated annual staff time consumed by each service by the access channel the service is delivered through via the staff utilisation workstream
7. Format for documenting the process and quality sign off requirements for this workstream

Deliverable

1. Annual staff overhead costs allocated to each service based on the access channel used for service delivery
2. Documentation outlining the process – this might include assumptions, work arounds, stakeholder consultations, calculations, data matching algorithms, caveats, data quality ratings, and quality sign off documentation

Streamlined employee cost calculation

- Employee costs = (average salary per FTE + annual estimate overhead costs per FTE, expressed as a salary percentage) × the number of employees in the department

The above calculation calculates employee costs. If used, the data quality ranking for employee cost should be set to three stars, because the calculation is based on evidence but the evidence isn't nuanced enough to take into account the costs variabilities. For a more nuanced approach, calculate indirect and on cost separately. Use the information below as a guide and revise the data quality ranking.

Guidance

Some core business systems record the time that staff spend on each task. Where this is not the case and/or where the data is patchy, the information can be estimated by conducting workshops or interviews with representative stakeholders to agree time proportions. It can also be achieved by asking front line and back-office staff to conduct a tick sheet exercise to mark off items, tasks, or observations as they are completed. The objective being to calculate the proportion of time spent delivering each service within scope. To increase the data quality rating, consider doing both.

The following table shows how these costs are calculated, data sources, and where the data should be entered in the business model. If the calculation includes more than one category of staff (e.g. front-office, back-office, or fulfilment), record the figures separately, unless they fall under the same cost centre and are not divisible. Use predictive analytics and/or 'what if' scenarios to model future staff reductions, pay rises, and known changes to the cost base. This workstream has dependencies from other workstreams.

Calculating costs

Calculation type	Data and calculations	What is included in this cost element	Suggested data sources	CTS formula reference
FTEs per service Conversion of part-time staff into FTEs.	Annual productive hours worked by full-time employees **divided by** annual hours per FTE per annum.	• Headcount per service • Number of hours worked per employee • Standard full-time hours	• HR system • Payroll data • Agency staff data	FTEs per service or department needed for annual productive minutes calculation.

Calculation type	Data and calculations	What is included in this cost element	Suggested data sources	CTS formula reference
Average salary per FTE This is derived by dividing the total salary paid to all employees in a business unit or department by the total number of employees in the business unit or department.	Total annual salary for the business unit **divided by** the number of FTEs in the business unit. This calculation takes management overheads into account.	• Number of FTEs per business unit • Annual budget for the business unit	• HR system • Payroll data • Agency staff data • General ledger	Average annual salary.
***Assumed staff utilisation per service** This reflects the percentage of time an employee has available to perform their duties or the duty being measured.	Percentage of time spent performing a particular task (e.g. 35% front office, 55% back office, and 10% for meetings, training, and miscellaneous activities).	Employees may work across more than one service, or they may not be fully engaged on a single task. Where this is the case, allocate their time to each task as a percentage.	• Business unit managers • Business unit staff • Telephone switch data • Case management business systems • Tick sheet data	Utilisation.
Average annual productive minutes per FTE The total amount of time an employee spends actively working or producing something each year.	Average annual hours per FTE calculated by multiplying the total number of minutes available in a year by staff utilisation expressed as a percentage.	• Number of FTEs per service • Average annual hours per FTE per service	To calculate the average annual minutes, divide the average annual hours by 60 and then multiply it by the number of FTEs.	Annual productive minutes per FTE.

***Explanation of assumed staff utilisation** – Consider this scenario: a business unit offers two distinct but related services, employing a total of four staff members, one of whom works part time. To determine staff utilisation, we will account for the part-time staff by considering them as 0.3 FTE. We can calculate the estimated utilisation for each service based on a 40-hour work week. Although utilisation is not a deliverable for this workstream, it is included here to demonstrate how the FTE calculation will be used.

Dept	Business unit	Grade	FTE	Staff No	Staff utilisation	
					Service 1	Service 2
Dept A	BU 123	8	1	12345	40%	20%
Dept A	BU 123	6	1	45678	60%	20%
Dept A	BU 123	5	1	67890	60%	20%
Dept A	BU 123	5	0.3	34567	100%	0%
Total			3.3	4	76 hrs/wk.	32 hrs/wk.

Calculation example

Annualised transactions, average annual salaries per grade, and the staff utilisation per service will play a crucial role in formulating the cost to serve calculation. The calculation for total staff time might look like this.

Service	FTEs	Annual productive minutes per FTE	Average productive minutes per department	Average annual salary per FTE	Average annual salary per department	Estimated utilisation	Data quality ranking
Food premises application	3.3	=523,200	=523,200*3.3	= Average annual salary per FTE	= Average annual salary per *3.3	65%	
Food premises renewal	3.3	=523,200	=523,200*3.3	= Average annual salary per FTE	= Average annual salary *3.3	20%	
Another licence	10	=523,200	=523,200*10	= Average annual salary per FTE	= Average annual salary *10	90%	

Subtotals might include:

- Department | Environment
- Service area | Business services
- Sub service | Licensing
- Service | Food premises registration application
- Service | Food premises registration renewal

Overheads calculations

Overhead costs are expenses that are not related to producing goods or services but are necessary to keep a business running. These costs are incurred by a business regardless of the number of sales it generates and can be either fixed or variable. Overheads can be calculated for each service delivery location because accommodation is often a significant overhead cost. Apportioning workspace can be done based on square meterage or staff numbers. Each approach has its advantages and disadvantages.

Apportioning office space by square metre

Advantages

- Fairness: Allocating cost based on square meterage ensures that accommodation overheads are based on team size.
- Flexibility: This method allows for flexibility in assigning cost based on specific requirements. For example, teams that require more equipment or storage space can be allocated a larger area with corresponding costs.

Disadvantages

- Inefficient space utilisation: Allocating team cost solely based on historic accommodation size can lead to space underutilisation, limiting availability for other parts of the business that could benefit from using the space.
- Lack of alignment with workflow: The distribution of workspace based on square meterage may not align with the actual workflow or collaboration needs of teams. It could hinder communication where teams that need to work closely together are physically separated.

Apportioning office space by staff numbers

Advantages

- Cost efficiency: Allocating accommodation costs based on FTE staff numbers can drive efficiency by enabling practices like mixed use and hotdesking. This approach facilitates shared workstations and flexible seating arrangements, resulting in reduced square meterage, lowered real estate costs, and decreased cost per head for accommodation.
- Collaboration and communication: Allocating space to employees from different teams that would benefit from working collaboratively can increase communication and productivity.
- Transparent and easy to manage: This method is based on a simple count of FTE employees, making it transparent and easy to manage and adjust as the organisation evolves.

Disadvantages

- Inequitable distribution: Allocating costs solely based on staff numbers may result in inequitable distribution. Different teams or departments may have different space requirements, and allocating cost per employee may not reflect the true costs of a department's space requirements.

In practice, a combination of both methods might be the best approach. For the purposes of this book, we use staff numbers as a baseline and treat specific space requirements as a channel cost. This allows for a fair distribution of costs while accommodating the varying requirements of distinct functions within the organisation.

Calculation type	Data and calculation	What is included in this cost element	Suggested data sources	CTS formula reference
Property cost per FTE per head The total cost of the building housing the service divided by the number of FTE employees and contractors who use/ occupy the property.	Property cost per head = Total property budget **divided by** the number of FTE staff who use or occupy the property.	• Rent or mortgage • Property taxes • Energy costs • Premises and ground maintenance • Security • Leases • Water and sewage • Cleaning	• General ledger property cost centres • Departmental property budget • No. of staff in a department – from HR system • No. of agency staff in a department	Property cost per FTE
Direct employee costs per FTE per head per business unit This relates to the total cost of employing an individual. Group employee costs by department, business unit, service, or function.	Direct employee costs = Total direct employee cost per business unit **divided by** the number of FTE staff in the business unit, with apportioned management cost.	Employment related expenses including salaries/wages, payroll taxes, employee benefits, paid holidays, holidays, apportioned management costs, bonuses and incentives.	• HR system • Payroll system • General ledger	Direct costs per FTE.
Indirect employee cost per FTE per head Expenses that are not related to an employee's salary or wages but are still incurred because of having an employee on staff. These costs can be either variable or fixed and can include a wide range of expenses.	Overheads incurred by employing a FTE member of staff for the organisation **divided by** the number of employees in the organisation.	Includes management overheads, employer paid taxes, sick pay, pensions, recruitment, training, legal fees, insurances & employee benefits.	• General ledger extract of indirect costs • No. of FTE staff	Indirect cost per FTE.
On-costs per FTE Costs added to the delivery of a service such as travel, stationary, PCs, and phones.	Total on cost for the business unit **divided by** the number of FTEs.	• Phones • Tablets • Computers • Software subscriptions	• General ledger	On-costs per FTE.

The following headings are an example of what the outputs might look like.

Service	(a) No. of FTEs	(b) Property costs per FTE	(c) Direct employee costs per FTE	(d) Indirect costs per FTE	(e) On costs per FTE	(f) Total cost per FTE
						(b+c+d+e) *a

Suggested data mapping for full time equivalent calculation

Requirements: A mapping from the cost centre hierarchy to departments and business units, the staff that work within the business units, and the salaries that they receive.

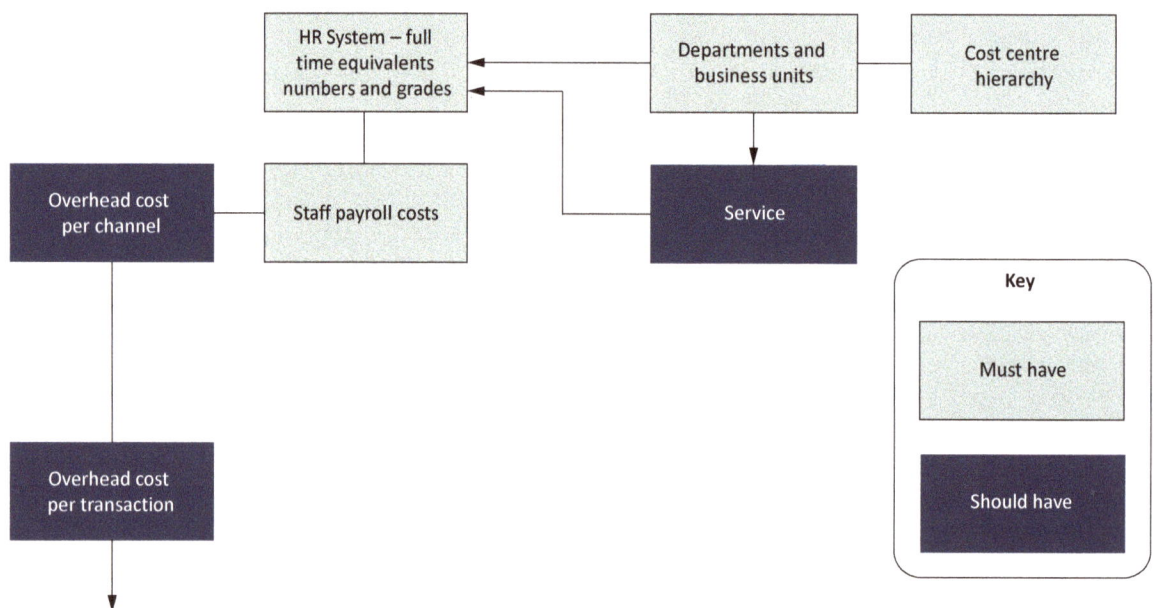

Quality sign-off

The quality sign-off of the approach and assumptions will require validation and sign-off by a senior responsible stakeholder.

5.4 Staff utilisation

The purpose of the project is to identify the average cost for delivering each service within the scope of the exercise.

The main purpose of this workstream is to:

1. Calculate the time staff spend delivering a service, where automated time recording does not exist and particularly where staff work on more than one process or in more than one service area (should have)

2. Calculate the opportunity cost of choosing one staffing scenario over another, by collecting data to support predictive analytics and 'what if' scenario planning (could have).

Requirements

The outputs from the staffing and costs workstream which will provide a business unit breakdown detailing the numbers of full-time equivalent staff with corresponding grades, mapped to cost centres.

Prerequisites

From the project manager you will receive:

1. The project scope

2. The depth of the analysis required

3. The organisational objectives in relation to this project

4. An overview of all the workstreams

5. Outputs from the customer interactions workstream

6. Outputs from the staffing and costs workstream

7. Data quality standards recording guidance

8. Formats for documenting the process and quality sign-off requirements

Deliverables

1. Assumed full-time equivalent staff (FTE), utilisation per service – proportion of FTE available time spent on delivering each service

2. Opportunity costs – proportion of FTE time spent by experts on work that could safely be conducted by generic staff

3. Quality sign-off by relevant stakeholders or stakeholder boards

4. Documentation outlining the process – this might include assumptions, work arounds, stakeholder consultations, calculations, data matching algorithms, caveats, data quality ratings, and quality sign-off documentation (must have)

Guidance

The purpose of this exercise is to calculate the amount of time staff spend delivering a service/ unit of production. With the right data points, it is possible to calculate this information without making assumptions. Both assumed and computer-generated staff utilisation calculations can be used in the dashboard. Assumed staff utilisation incorporates the aspects of working in the environment that a calculation alone cannot capture. Attention should be paid to where there is a significant difference between the two. To arrive at as close to the true assumed time spent delivering a service, where automated time recording does not exist and where staff work on more than one process or in more than one service area, it will be necessary to estimate the average proportion of time staff spend in each area. For example, four members of staff provide support for four related but distinct service offerings, they also have a manager who is responsible for other service areas, the manager supports their service area for 20% of the available time. To determine how service staff split their time to meet demands, you may need them to collaborate with each other and their manager to agree time proportions. Cost estimations should take the cost of the manager's time into account.

In the following example, the types of licences processed are counted, but not the contact reasons. In scenarios like these, consider using tick sheets to estimate the proportion of time spent on more granular service request types and annualise the results.

Level 1	Level 2	Level 3	FTE Count	% of time spent delivering service
Environment	Licences	Food premises registration	1.2	37%
Environment	Licences	Premises licence	1.4	43%
Environment	Licences	Skip licence	0.4	7.5%
Environment	Licences	Street trading	1	12.5%

One might naturally be inclined to focus on reducing the time spent on servicing food registration and premises licences, given that providing these services consumes 80% of staff time. However, to develop more nuanced targeted interventions, consider taking service groupings for expensive to run and high-volume services one step further to Level 4. Examples of Level 4 interactions include applying for a licence, renewing a licence, complaining about the process or experience, appealing a decision, and making status enquiries. The gems are in the detail. In the example below, 28% of four FTE staff members' time is spent responding to status enquiries. With a CTS implementation one could calculate what the savings would be if status enquiries were significantly reduced by redesigning the service to manage expectations so that most customers either did not feel the need to request an update, updates were automated, or customers could self-serve.

Business unit details					Level 4, assumed staff utilisation %				
Level 1 Name	Level 2	Level 3	FTE count	Annual volumes	Apply	Renew	Complain	Appeal	Status enquiry
Environment	Licences	Food registration	1.2	1,149	8%	10%	1%	6%	12%
Environment	Licences	Premises licence	1.4	852	5%	11%	1%	13%	13%
Environment	Licences	Skip licence	0.4	900	3%	2%	0.5%	0.0%	2%
Environment	Licences	Street trading	1	63	2%	7.5%	1.5%	0.5%	1%

A further iteration could look at the 19.5% of staff time used to service appeals. What if the top reasons for failed applications were publicised with the guidance, could this increase the number of customers getting it right the first time and reduce the number of customers making futile appeals, saving even more time? You may wish to consider using A/B testing to assess the efficacy of different scenarios and at the same time check for service transference (e.g. whether a reduction in appeals equates to increased demand elsewhere, like complaints or licence infringement checks).

Staff utilisation is a metric of equal significance to staff costs, as it offers additional data points and more nuanced insights. This information not only enhances our ability to report effectively but also provides valuable options for refining processes and designing for efficiency with greater precision.

5.41 Opportunity cost

Opportunity cost is a concept in economics and decision making, emphasising that resources are scarce, and choosing one option over another involves trade-offs. The concept is applicable in various contexts, however, the context being addressed here is the balance between using skilled professional staff to fulfil the entirety of their role, versus using trained support staff to fulfil the more repetitive functions. Examples of this might be reducing administrative support and requiring skilled professionals to conduct their own administration, or using more administrative staff and fewer expensive professionals. In principle, requiring skilled staff to carry out their own administration works as a cost reduction initiative, but there may be a tipping point beyond which demand is unmet or there is a demand backlog accentuated by the proportion of time it takes a professional to carry the administrative workload, thereby reducing the organisation's capacity to deliver enough units of work to meet demand.

'What if' scenarios could be employed to calculate the optimal cost and staff ratios that would meet demand without significant staff, over or underutilisation. Administrative support, strategically used in these scenarios, can help balance the workload and reduce revenue costs without compromising quality. While the measurement of opportunity cost is undeniably subjective, it can prove useful as an indication of where a co-design stakeholder workshop might be beneficial to explore the possibilities.

Measuring opportunity cost

To measure the optimisation of the balance between administrative tasks and expert input, it will be necessary to agree on two definitions:

1. The roles that expert staff occupy

2. Definitions of administrative tasks

The term 'expert or professional staff' is used to describe individuals who exhibit an elevated level of knowledge, qualifications, skill, or proficiency in a particular field, subject matter, or domain. This designation implies a degree of proficiency that surpasses the standard or average within the organisation. Expert staff members are specifically recruited for their expertise and experience, they should therefore be identifiable by their job titles and the specifications for their roles.

To identify the administrative tasks that experts and non-experts might undertake, it will be necessary to agree a definition of the functions and use these definitions as part of the staff utilisation discovery workshop. Depending on your context, it may be necessary to include manual roles that require physical strength, dexterity, and practical skills, within either the expert or non-expert definitions. Suggestions for identifying administrative tasks are given below.

Suggested administrative function definitions

Support and coordination	Operations management
1. Arranging transportation	18. Appeal management
2. Booking resources	19. Case management and processing
3. Inbox management	20. Checking and chasing
4. Internal communications	21. Customer communications
5. Financial administration	22. Customer support
6. Managing diaries	23. Complaints management
7. Managing events	24. Contract management
8. Organising meetings	25. Data checking/validation
9. Organising conferences	26. Data entry
10. Photocopying and scanning	27. Dealing with payments and/or refunds
11. Posting and packing	28. Dealing with customer enquiries
12. Procurement	29. Document archiving
13. Reception duties	30. Document preparation and processing
14. Recruitment administration	31. Issuing passes, permits, licences, or certificates
15. Stationary management	32. Order taking and processing
16. Taking and producing minutes	33. Payments and refunds
17. Transporting and/or delivering	34. Routine health and safety and training

There are four additional questions that should be added to the staff utilisation data gathering exercise to capture information, which will support 'what if' scenario analysis. They are:

1. Is the role professional or generic?

2. What percentage of the role is dedicated to performing one or more of the defined functions that you believe could safely be conducted by non-experts, utilising safety checks to minimise the necessity for experts to review and rework the outputs?

3. Is there a backlog of work that exceeds service level agreement limits? If so, what is the current count of units of work in the backlog?

4. If new units of work ceased, how much time would be required to clear the existing backlog?

With the example below, including annual transactions and annual average transaction will enable the calculation of the number of days required to clear the backlog. This data can be used for 'what if' scenarios to determine the optimal balance of staff costs to meet customer demand.

Business unit information				Staff utilisation		Opportunity cost indicator			
1. Role	2. Grade	3. Number of staff	4. Average pay scale	5. Service 1, e.g. customer service	6. Service 2, e.g. back office	7. Is the role mainly admin?	8. % of time spent on admin?	9. Back log units of work outside SLA	10. No. of days to clear backlog
ABC	8	9	11	90%	10%	No	35%	287	29
LMN	7	6	10	85%	15%	No	20%	31	6
XYZ	5	2	6	20%	80%	Yes	90%	24	5

Suggested data map for staff utilisation workstream

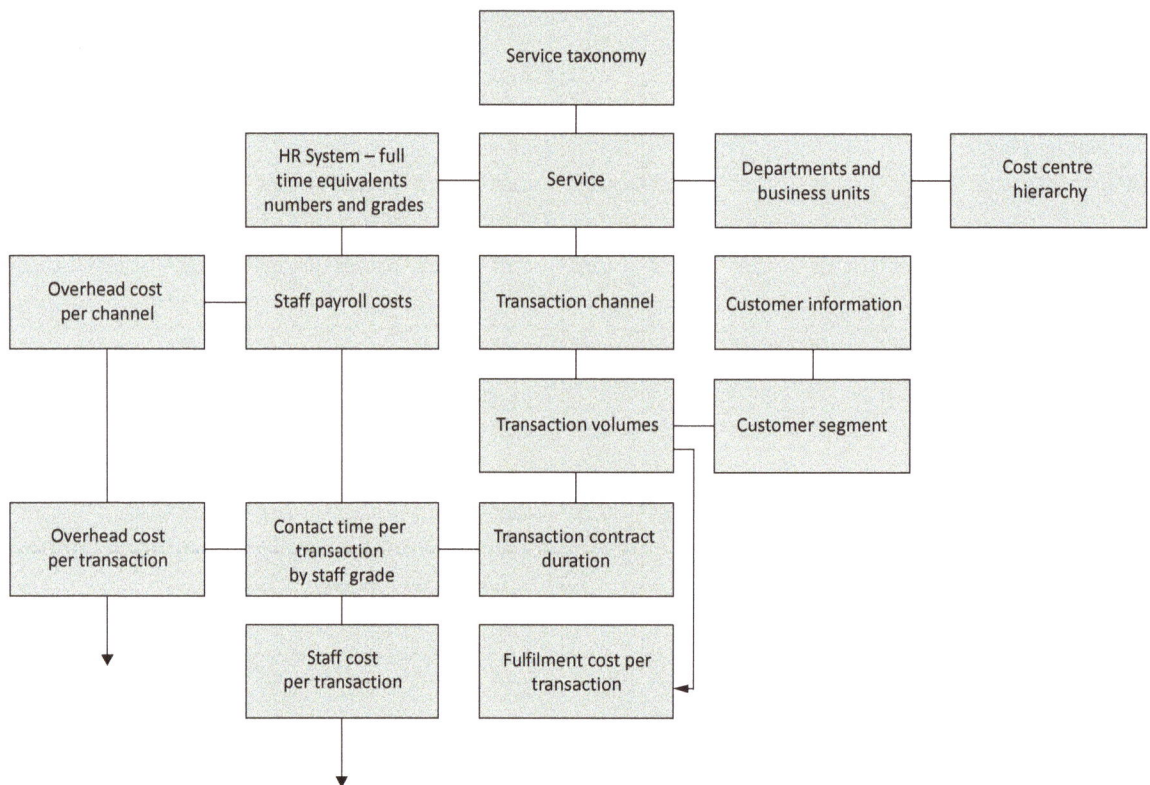

5.5 Access channels workstream

An access channel refers to a means or path through which individuals, devices, or entities can interact with or gain entry to a particular service or resource. These channels typically include web, telephone, face-to-face, and other modes of service access.

Objective

The purpose of the project is to identify the average cost for delivering each service within the scope of the exercise.

The purpose of this workstream is to:

- Identify the access channels within scope
- Establish the number of transactions handled by each channel for each service

- Calculate the average transaction cost associated with the use of each access channel for each service

Main Deliverables

1. A list of access channels within scope

2. Calculation of channel costs per transaction for each service or service grouping

3. Documentation outlining the process – this might include assumptions, work arounds, stakeholder consultations, calculations, data matching algorithms, caveats, data quality ratings, and quality sign off documentation

Prerequisites

From the project manager you will receive:

1. The project scope

2. The depth of the analysis required

3. The organisational objectives in relation to this project

4. Data quality standards recording guidance

5. An overview of all the workstreams

6. Documented process, assumptions, work arounds, stakeholders consulted, and caveats for this workstream.

Streamlined channel cost

Channel cost per transaction = annual channel cost/annual channel transactions

The channel cost is calculated as the annual channel cost divided by annual channel transactions – simple and straightforward. However, as is often the case, there are additional layers of complexity. If the above calculation is applied to all services, the data quality ranking for channel cost should be set to three stars. This is because the calculation is based on evidence, but the evidence lacks nuance to consider the variability of the services included.

For a more nuanced approach and to ensure all access channels (payment systems, chatbots, social media channels, etc.) are considered, use the information below as a guide. Select the relevant areas and revise the data quality ranking accordingly.

Guidance

Having decided on the services that are in scope from the customer transactions, identify the access channels that those services are delivered through. For the purposes of this exercise, back-office processing costs are managed in the same way as customer access channels. You may find the following list helpful.

Select the access channels that apply to your organisation or add your own.

| D: Digital channels, digital inbound and outbound self-service channels | S: Support channels | B: Back-office channels | L: Legacy channels |

✓	Ref	Access channels	Description
	D1	Web – providing information	Navigation, information, help, feedback, FAQs
	D2	Web – transactions	Online accounts, eForms, case management and eCommunications
	D3	Online Payment	Payment via web form
	D4	SMS/email transactions	Reminders, personalised nudges, verification, surveys, feedback, password resets and payments – outbound only
	D5	Video call	Customer meetings

✓	Ref	Access channels	Description
	D6	Social media (communications)	Communications, marketing linked to content from approved sources and signposting
	D7	Explainer video	Invitation, nudge, reminder, and 1st line self-service support channels
	D8	Chatbot	To address common issues, FAQs and out of hours support, automated and promoted at the point of need.
	D9	App	Dedicated personal account app
	S1	Email	Unstructured customer contact or used for back-office comms
	S2	Social media (support)	Monitor, invite user to alternative channel where relevant and link relevant cases to CRM
	S3	Live chat	One-on-one support to guide customers within their digital journey
	S4	Call centre with IVR	Support channel and transactional where the need arises
	S5	Click to call	Online access to the telephone support channel at the point of need
	S6	Face-to-face	Appointments, drop-in surgeries, and other customer access points
	S7	Post/bulk scanning	Letters/forms scanned indexed and uploaded for case management
	S8	Assisted digital face-to-face support	Support for the digitally excluded to access services via an intermediary
	S9	Accessibility support	On demand easy read, descriptive text, audio, digital braille, braille, and translations
	B1	Back office	Overall management and processing of service requests
	B2	Fulfilment	Goods, picking, packing, shipping, delivery, installation, maintenance, repairs, etc.
	L1	Letters/paper forms/fax	Promoted only when the customer journey or need arises
	L2	Telephone non IVR	Data from this source should not be giving a data quality rating that is higher than two stars

Comprehensive channel costs

Access channels include web transactions, telephone contact centres, face-to-face transactions and the like. These calculations will allow your organisation to compare the cost of delivering services via different access channels and is essential for identifying touch points that trigger an increase in channel hopping behaviour, the efficacy of interventions employed to keep customers using self-service pathways, and the benefits of channel shift. If channel costs are likely to change, use predictive analytics if past data is available and/or 'what if' scenario analysis to explore future possibilities.

Every organisation has its own way of calculating costs, therefore my advice is that you should do it your way, all you need to do is record and defend the process, which should incorporate the costs listed below (if there is not a good reason for exclusion). The following information is provided for guidance.

5.51 Fixed access channel costs

Fixed channel costs refer to expenses that are associated with maintaining a communication channel or medium that a business or organisation uses to serve, sell, or otherwise communicate with its customers or clients. The costs shown in the following table are typically fixed in nature, which means they do not vary with the amount of usage of the communication channel.

Examples of fixed channel costs include the fees associated with obtaining and maintaining a telephone system, renting or leasing a physical customer walk-in space, the basic cost of software as a service (SaaS), front- and back-office systems, the fees for maintaining a website and other platforms used to support channel specific transactions, and the proportional cost of the staff recruited to maintain them (e.g. digital web teams, system support, outsourced support, etc).

Use the process throughput map from the customer transactions workstream to map fixed channel costs across customer journeys. The following example shows the web cost used by all channels to complete a process. In this example, the systems used to complete a transaction are not integrated, so the average cost per transaction is captured for each system.

Service identifiers				System cost per transaction				
Level 1 Name	Level 2 Name	Level 3 Name	Level 3 Attribute	System 1 CRM	System 2 Apply	System 3 Payment	System 4 Complain	Back-office time
Environment	Licences	Food premises registration	Apply	0.01	0.15	0.20		
Environment	Licences	Food premises registration	Complain	0.01			0.35	
Environment	Licences	Food premises registration	Appeal	0.01				20 mins, 20× *FTE/min cost
Environment	Licences	Food premises registration	Status enquiry	0.01				4 mins, 4× *FTE/min cost

*Full time equivalent

5.52 Variable access channel costs

Variable channel costs are the costs incurred when a company or organisation distributes its products or services through different channels. These costs vary depending on the channel used and can include expenses such as the cost of making a service more accessible by providing alternative pathways and accessible formats, printing, packaging, postage, handling, and the processing of inbound paper communications etc. Variable channel costs are an important consideration in determining the most profitable and efficient distribution strategy for a business, or the cost for making a service more accessible to its client base.

5.53 Back-office costs

With respect to calculating the cost to serve, the back office should be treated as an access channel. A back-office process refers to an operational activity that provides the administration necessary for fulfilling a customer service request, originating from a front-office channel. Where the process differs by service request type, the processing cost is likely to differ, and it follows that cost will differ too. Therefore, depending on the level of granularity required, it may be necessary to calculate average back-office processing minutes per service request type.

Calculating back-office processing costs per transaction involves determining the total expenses incurred in performing back-office operations and dividing it by the number of transactions processed within a specific period. To do this we can use the same method used for calculating staff and channel costs.

5.54 Back-office wait time and transport time

Lean methodology is an approach that focuses on doing more with less, it helps businesses to organise and optimise how they do things so they can work more efficiently and save time and resources. One of the aims of Lean methodology is to minimise or eliminate both transport and wait times by optimising the flow of materials, information, and labour through the process. Wait time and transport time are not required for the cost to serve, but they are of interest to service transaction analytics. For this reason, you should consider naming and recording wait and transport times within a process while you are measuring the contact time. Examples of wait time names might be 'Food premises registration – awaiting payment confirmation', 'Food premises registration – processing backlog', or 'Food premises registration – awaiting committee decision'. Giving the wait and transport times names that relate to the process provides a standard for measuring change over time. Collecting this information will provide a valuable data point for your transaction analytics dashboard.

5.55 Fixed back-office processing costs

Fixed channel costs refer to the fixed expenses that are associated with processing the service requests. For the purposes of the calculation, it should be treated as a channel cost.

Examples of fixed processing costs might include the fees associated with obtaining and maintaining the line of business system, facilities used to support processing, including telephone systems, and other platforms used to process the transaction.

5.56 Variable back-office processing costs

Variable channel costs are the costs incurred by the back office. Examples include scanning, photocopying, printing, postage, and the handling and processing of inbound paper communications.

5.57 Channel calculations

When multiple services use an access channel, the cost associated with that channel should be allocated to each service proportionally, based on the percentage of transaction volumes.

- Channel cost per transaction = annual channel cost/annual channel transactions

Divide the annual channel cost by the annual channel transactions for each service to arrive at the channel cost per transaction. See the table below for examples.

Name	Description	Calculation	Suggested data source	Formula reference
Annual fixed channel cost	Expenses associated with maintaining a channel used to serve, sell, or otherwise communicate with customers	To calculate fixed cost per transaction for a specific channel, divide the fixed channel costs by the annual number of transactions processed through that channel for the organisation	• Contracts • General ledger	Fixed channel costs
Variable channel costs	Expenses associated with delivering a specific product, service, or service group	To calculate variable cost per transaction, divide the variable channel costs by the annual number of related transactions processed through the channel	• Transaction records • Variable costs accessibility contracts • Distribution costs (postage etc.) • SMS/email notifications	Variable channel costs

Name	Description	Calculation	Suggested data source	Formula reference
Annual fixed processing costs	Fixed expenses associated with the back office processing the service request	To calculate fixed back-office processing cost per transaction, divide the annual processing costs by the number of transactions processed through line of business systems during the same period	• Contracts • General ledger	Fixed processing costs
Annual variable processing costs	Variable expenses associated with the back-office processing of the service request	To calculate variable back-office processing cost per transaction, divide the variable processing costs by the annual number of transactions	• Line of business systems • Distribution costs (postage etc.) • SMS/email/letter notifications	Variable processing costs

Now we have the unit cost for every transaction we can work out the proportion of the channel costs that should be allocated to each service. Multiply the estimated channel cost per transaction by the number of transactions for each service to arrive at the proportional channel cost for each service.

Channel _____   Annual channel cost £_____

Service	No of transactions	Estimated channel costs per transaction	Annual channel cost for service
Food premises application	800	£0.08	£64

Channel costs per transaction

The transaction record is likely to contain the service name, the date and time of the interaction, and for the telephone it is likely to include the call duration. Summarise the information for each service and access channel so that every record contains service identifiers, the access channel, annual or estimated annual volumes, and annual average transaction durations. Consider investigating extreme outliers with the aim of potentially excluding them from the standard calculation and, if they are an area for concern, investigating them separately.

#	Service	Annual channel transactions	Fixed channel cost per transaction	Variable channel cost per transaction	Average channel cost per transaction	Average channel costs / transaction / annum	Data quality ranking
	Licence application	1,000	0.30	0.70	0.30+0.70	1000x(0.30+0.70)	
	Licence renewal	1,000	0.30		0.30	1000x0.30	

Calculation **including** variable channel costs.

Calculation **excluding** variable channel costs.

Suggested data map for the access channels workstream

Map cost centres to business units, business units to access channels costs, and access channel costs to channel transaction volumes. Costs can be mapped at a business unit level or at service levels, depending on the granularity of the requirements.

Quality sign-off

For quality, ensure that the approach is signed off by a senior finance stakeholder and/or the person responsible for managing the contract(s). For repeatability, the signed off document should be kept with the audit trail, which should include the approach taken, assumptions, inclusions, and exclusions.

Section 3: Consolidating the results

6.0 Data management workstream: repositories, dashboards and calculations

Objective

The purpose of the project is to identify the average cost for delivering each service within the scope of the exercise.

The purpose of this workstream is to design a service transaction data repository and create drillable dashboards for calculating the cost to serve, staff utilisation, and the opportunity cost associated with choosing one method of delivering services over another. These dashboards will be applicable to the organisation, as well as departments, business units, and services.

You will need

The outputs from every workstream.

Prerequisites

From the project manager you will receive:

1. The project scope
2. The depth of the analysis required
3. The organisational objectives in relation to this project
4. Data quality standards recording guidance
5. A list of the workstreams and their outputs

Deliverables

1. Data repository
2. Drillable dashboard
3. Cost to serve calculations
4. Balanced scorecard containing baseline data
5. Documentation, designed to walk a new member of staff through the process

6.1 Dashboards

In their paper 'The Hidden Cost of Cost-to-Serve', Seifert and Markoff (2018) argue that the benefits can be unclear because data collation 'is rarely applied in a sustainable, repeatable way'. The objective of this workstream is to establish a sustainable and repeatable data repository while thoroughly documenting the process. The documentation should outline the standards for data collection and cleansing, and, should be stored in an updatable format, preferably with an audit trail. Cataloguing will keep track of changes and the rationale for making those changes.

The tools, capability, and complexity of your cost to serve data repository should be tailored to your requirements. It is crucial to recognise this as a strategic tool that plays a multifaceted role, guiding financial decisions and enabling businesses to navigate towards efficiency and profitability. This tool provides analysts with the means to paint a clear picture of costs, adding depth to financial insights. If well structured, it serves as a foundation for current and future informed decision making.

Your responsibility is to shape the data standards, either construct a new data repository, or integrate this data into an existing one. Your task includes creating a diagram illustrating data flows, facilitating the sharing of the mapping of data entities utilised in constructing the dashboard, and assessing the agreed-upon KPIs. A broad overview of potential data entities is presented here as a reference guide.

Suggested map of data requirements

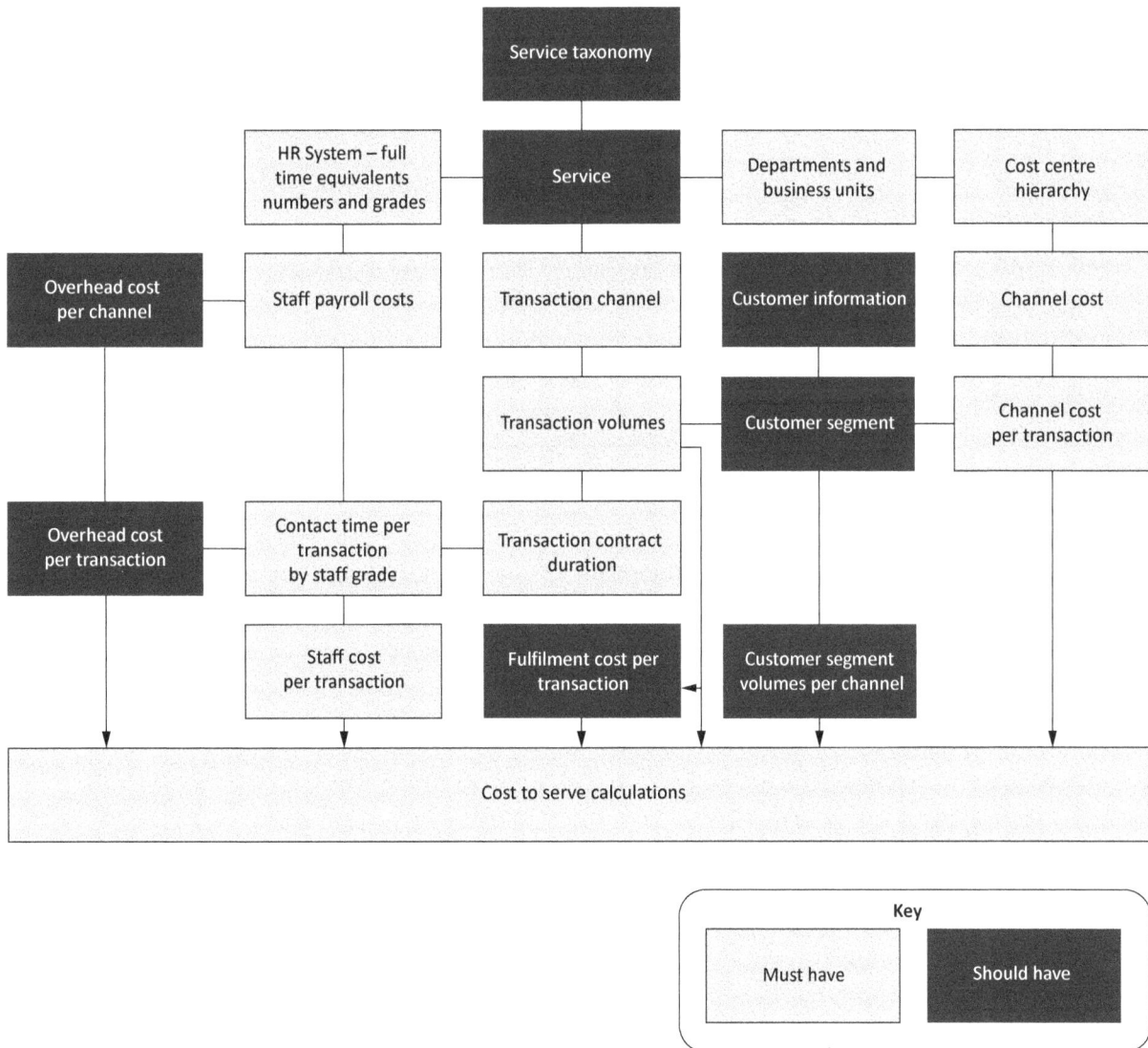

Guidance

This is an important aspect of the project: the guidance on how to construct the dashboard cannot come from this text, but from the vision. Consider holding a vision workshop to imagine and rank the deliverables. The following is provided as a guide.

1. User understanding

- Consider the diverse audience who will use the dashboard

- Ensure that the dashboard aligns with their varied levels of expertise and responsibilities

2. **Key metrics and KPIs**

    ○ Identify the critical metrics and KPIs relevant to cost to serve

    ○ Determine the hierarchy or tiers of importance for these metrics

3. **Data granularity**

    ○ Define the level of detail or granularity required for effective analysis, e.g. ability to capture transaction data at the granular level of date and time.

    ○ Consider how drilldowns will enhance understanding without overwhelming users

4. **User interaction**

    ○ Encourage user interactivity through drilldowns and filters

    ○ Allow users to customise views to meet their specific needs

5. **Data quality and consistency**

    ○ Ensure that data sources are reliable and consistent

    ○ Document data cleansing and validation processes

6. **Scalability and performance**

    ○ Design the dashboard with scalability in mind to accommodate future data growth

    ○ Optimise performance, particularly for multitiered and drillable features

7. **User training and support**

    ○ Develop user guides, communities, or practice, or provide training sessions to familiarise users with the dashboard

    ○ Establish a support system for addressing queries or issues

    ○ Consider embedding intervention decision support tools that allow the user to look at the return on investment against effort, time, risks, dependencies, cost, and net present value

8. **Feedback mechanism**

    ○ Implement a feedback mechanism to collect user insights for continuous improvement

    ○ Allow users to suggest enhancements or modifications

9. **Security and access control**

    ○ Consider data security and implement access controls to ensure sensitive information is protected

    ○ Differentiate access levels based on user roles and responsibilities

10. **Integration with existing systems**

    ○ Assess compatibility with existing systems and technologies

    ○ Ensure seamless integration for a cohesive data environment

    ○ Consider integration with customer segmentation data

11. **Desired capabilities**

    ○ Ability to perform or support 'what if' scenarios and predictive analytics

    ○ Ability to upload batch data

    ○ Ability to record the initiation and cessation dates of interventions, as well as capturing transaction data at the granular level of date and time

12. **Further considerations**

    ○ Steer clear of creating a single point of failure or a complex system that necessitates specialised analysts

    ○ Keep an eye out for double counting

6.2 Calculations

The dashboards will offer a drillable view of the data. The calculation for the cost to serve is based on a formula. Data for the calculations is collected by various workstreams, as listed below. Each data element should be accompanied by a data quality rating, indicating the level of confidence the business has in the accuracy or reliability of the data.

6.3 Summary of the data feeds for the cost to serve calculation

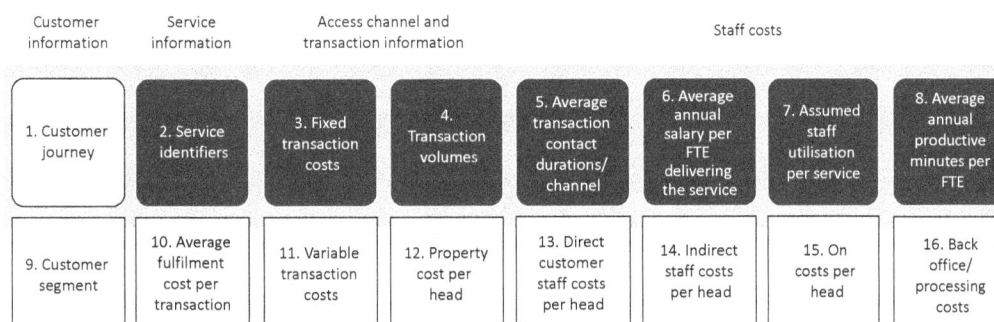

Customer information	Service information	Access channel and transaction information			Staff costs		
1. Customer journey	2. Service identifiers	3. Fixed transaction costs	4. Transaction volumes	5. Average transaction contact durations/ channel	6. Average annual salary per FTE delivering the service	7. Assumed staff utilisation per service	8. Average annual productive minutes per FTE
9. Customer segment	10. Average fulfilment cost per transaction	11. Variable transaction costs	12. Property cost per head	13. Direct customer staff costs per head	14. Indirect staff costs per head	15. On costs per head	16. Back office/ processing costs

1. **Customer journey/accessibility needs** – the journey assigned to the customer based on preference and need (access channels, accessibility support channels, omnichannel support).

2. **Service identifier** – a customer journey touchpoint reference identifying the service, the customer journey stage, and the interaction reason.

3. **Fixed annual channel costs for the access channel** – the method of access used for contact (e.g. online, call centre telephone, paper form, assisted digital, etc.). Includes outsourced contracts and maintenance costs that are independent of volumes and will not vary within a year.

4. **Transaction volumes** – the number of transactions for each service by access channel over a determined period.

5. **Average transaction duration** – average contact time spent by staff on behalf of the customer for each channel.

6. **Average annual salary per full-time equivalent (FTE)** – the salary of staff delivering the service.

7. **Assumed or calculated staff utilisation** – the percentage of available time staff spend delivering the service.

8. **Average annual productive minutes** – the annual number of minutes available per FTE to service customers, taking leave, sick leave, and training days into account.

9. **Customer segment** – the group that the customer statistically shares the most characteristics with.

10. **Average fulfilment cost per transaction** – the annual cost incurred to deliver the non-administrative portion of a particular service to customers, divided by the number of fulfilment transactions. Includes material costs, fulfilment labour costs, shipping costs, travel costs, and fulfilment overhead costs.

11. **Variable channel transaction costs** – costs associated with individual transaction volumes such as printing, posting, scanning, and faxing.

12. **Property cost per head** – the cost per head of providing the service from the building the service is delivered from.

13. **Direct staff costs** – costs that relate to labour (e.g. salaries, national insurance, pension contributions, honorariums, sick pay and overtime, agency staff and consultants, etc.).

14. **Indirect staff costs** – overheads that do not relate to the provision of the service, such as management overheads, recruitment, HR, finance, marketing, and training.

15. **On costs per head** – costs added to the delivery of a service such as travel, stationary, PCs, and phones.

16. **Back-office/processing costs** – cost of back-office processing and/or fulfilling the service request.

Total channel cost for each service

To calculate the total channel cost of delivering a single service to a customer, it is necessary to include on cost, and costs that are fixed, variable, direct and indirect. This approach includes the costs that are invisible because they are absorbed by the whole business or by a part of the business.

If this is not going to be a one-off analysis, there needs to be a process. Using the quality control framework, collect a list of who, how, why, data quality scores, and assumptions to design a process for cyclical collation of cost to serve data that can be compared against a baseline with the aim of automating as much of the process as possible over time, and ensuring the processes that are not automated are calculated in a repeatable and consistent manner.

Data requirements

Calculation: Annual transaction minutes = average transaction duration minutes × channel volumes

Data

- Front office annual transaction volumes per channel
- Front office annual average transaction duration minutes per channel
- Back office annual transaction volumes per channel
- Back office annual average transaction duration minutes per channel

Average Transaction Duration (Minutes)

Use a combination of mean, median, and mode to determine the best metric for identifying the typical length of staff contact time used to complete a given transaction.

Compare Mean and Median, if the mean and median are close:

- The data is likely to be symmetrically distributed, so the mean will provide a good estimate of the typical time.

- If the mean and median differ significantly, the data is likely to be skewed. In this case, the median is a better measure of the typical time. However before making a decision to use the median, consider using the mode.

Consider the Mode:

- If the data has a significant graphical peak, the mode can be a useful measure.
- If the data has multiple peaks, this might indicate multiple pathways, varying levels of staff experience, or a confusing access channel interface. if a service has multiple pathways, consider disaggregating them into separate services.

Staff Data

Calculation: Annual minutes available per FTE = staff utilisation x annual productive minutes/FTE

Data

- Number of FTE per service
- Number of productive minutes available per FTE
- Assumed and calculated staff utilisation %

Staff Costs

Calculation: Annual employee cost = average annual salary + direct cost per head + indirect cost per head + property cost per head + on cost per head

Data

- Average annual salary per head
- Direct cost per head
- Indirect cost per head
- Property cost per head
- On cost per head

Channel Costs

Calculation: Channel cost = annual fixed channel cost + annual variable channel * channel use percentage

Data

- Annual fixed channel cost
- Annual variable channel cost
- Annual proportion of channel use.

6.4 Cost to serve formula

Even fully automated processes are likely to include some human intervention, for example:

- when things go wrong
- where the request or circumstances are non-standard
- where adjustments need to be made to provide a true reflection of the circumstances

The following formula takes staff time into account.

Part 1a: Total channel cost: human intervention access channels

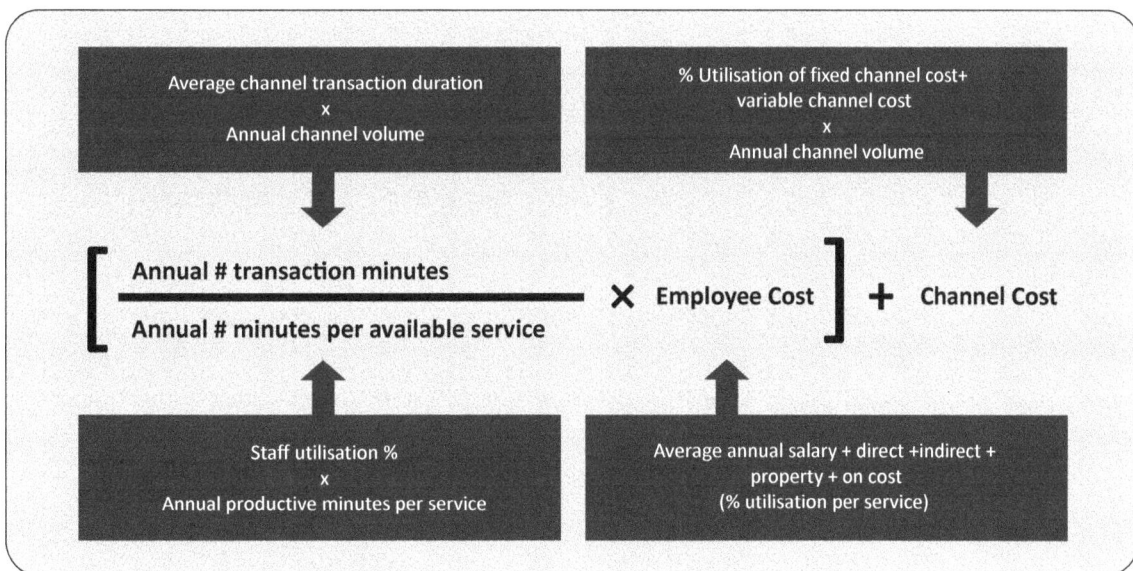

Part 1b: Total channel cost: web and self-service channels

For fully automated processes, use the formula below to calculate the cost of delivering services through self-service channels where transactions are completed without human intervention, in place of 1a above.

Part 1C: Average customer time: web and self-service channels

While customer time is not traditionally included in unpacking the organisational cost of providing a service, capturing the time customers spend engaging with your organisation in the process of obtaining a service yields valuable service improvement indicators. These indicators include measures of frustration levels, abandonment rates, increased utilisation of chatbots, and channel hopping.

a) Average time per transaction:

$$\text{Average time per transaction} = \frac{\text{Total time spent by customers}}{\text{Number of channel transactions}}$$

b) Average waiting time:

$$\text{Average waiting time} = \frac{\text{Total time customers spend waiting}}{\text{Number of customers}}$$

c) Customer time value:

$$\text{Customer time value} = \text{Average transaction value} \times \text{Average time spent per transaction}$$

Part 2: Cost per transaction

This final part of the calculation uses the 'total channel costs' computed in 1a or 1b above and divides the answer by the annual number of channel transactions to arrive at the cost to serve.

$$\text{Cost per service transaction} = \frac{\text{Total channel cost}}{\text{Annual number of channel transactions}}$$

6.5 Channel profitability

Channel profitability refers to the financial performance and profitability of different sales or distribution channels utilised by a business to reach its customers. It involves assessing the revenue generated, costs incurred, and overall profitability associated with each channel through which products or services are sold. There may be a marked difference between the profitability of individual services and channels. Self-service channels will, on the surface, generate more profit, but this should be mapped against back-office costs. The inefficient collection of self-service information can result in a higher cost for self-service channels where the self-service channel is not integrated with back-office systems or customers process their orders by a self-service channel but then make further contact for status updates and reassurance.

Profitability =

Total Channel Cost (including back-office costs) + total fulfilment cost + refunds + processing returns + bad debt + waste + customer support cost + depreciation + research and development + taxes + amount set aside for future liabilities.

Minus

Income

Where the outcome is a negative number, this represents the budget requirement, shortfall, or loss.

Identify, and flag for investigation, excessive cost outliers for the following components for each service or service group:

- front office processing cost
- back office processing cost
- the cost of processing returns
- bad debt
- waste
- customer support.

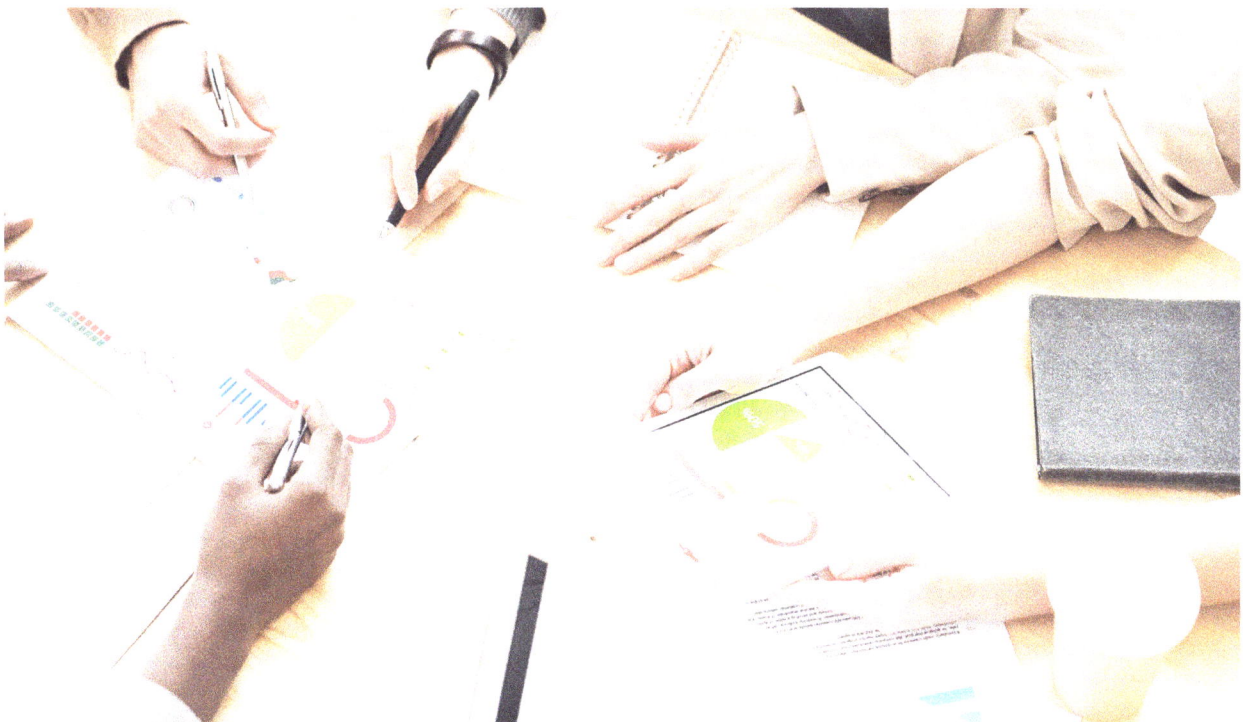

7.0 Exploring your data

Prioritise your business transformation initiatives, consider using an effort-benefit matrix. This tool will help you identify and prioritise projects that offer the greatest potential for reducing the cost to serve.

7.1 Evaluate your strengths

Bruce Barton (1927) in his book 'What can a man believe', ended his work with a story that has been retold many times, it goes something like this:

The great fire of 1666 destroyed the centre of London. It completely gutted St Paul's Cathedral. This event gave Sir Christopher Wren the opportunity to rebuild it. One morning he visited the site and observed the workers, most of whom did not know him, and of three men engaged in the same task he asked the question: "What are you doing?"

From the first man he received the answer "I am cutting this stone", from the second, the answer was "I am earning a living", but the third man, straightened up, squared his shoulders, and proudly replied "I am building a cathedral".

If as a leader you are going to embark on a cost to serve analytics exercise, you will need to understand the strengths of your travelling companions. A team lead who is 'cutting stone' is doing as they are told, if you do not hold the entire vision (which at this stage you are unlikely to do) then you may not be able to exploit the opportunities that a cost to serve repository could bestow from their input alone. If the outlook is 'earning a living', the job is a means to a non-career related end therefore, it may not be in such a person's interest to suggest anything that might increase their workload. You are really looking for cathedral builders but if there isn't a perfect fit, here are some of the considerations that will help you to steer the process.

By now, you might have a prioritised list of goals for this exercise and possibly a clear execution plan. If your plans are still in development, the information in the rest of this chapter will explore various possibilities and provide valuable insights to help you transform your cost-to-serve requirements into a concrete strategy and execution plan.

7.2 Scan the horizon

Horizon scanning is about looking ahead, much like a chess player anticipating future moves. By identifying trends, opportunities, and threats, you can craft strategies to stay ahead and gain a competitive edge. Consider the political, economic, social, technological, legal, and environmental landscapes. Look for emerging technologies and observe what others in your field—and beyond—are doing, to support you in making your decisions future-proof.

Explore offerings from product vendors, attend conferences, and listen to expert podcasts. Validate the applicability of your insights by discussing them with internal teams through ideation workshops, which help generate, develop, and explore ways to capitalize on your cost-to-serve analytics repository.

7.3 Consider lead and lag indicators

Lead indicators are predictive measures that give early signals about future performance, they are used to anticipate potential outcomes such as savings that could be realised because of reducing the cost to serve, estimated annual number of employee training hours, and failure demand reduction rates. They help anticipate potential outcomes and allow for proactive adjustments.

Lag indicators are outcome measures that reflect the results of past actions. They provide information on the effectiveness of strategies and initiatives after they have been implemented. Examples include the cost per transaction, which because it uses historical data, is a lag indicator. Another example is failure demand / repeat contact rates.

Using both lead and lag indicators together will allow your organisation to monitor predictive metrics, evaluate outcome metrics, and adjust strategies accordingly. This balance ensures continuous improvement in reducing service costs while maintaining or enhancing service quality and customer satisfaction.

7.4 Choose meaningful metrics for your dashboard

Meaningful metrics are clear and actionable pieces of information that guide you toward your goals, much like the essential controls and gauges in an airplane cockpit help the pilot take off, navigate, and land safely. While statistical metrics like mode, median, and standard deviation can provide an understanding of the overall operating environment, they are useful but not always directly actionable. Adjusting any of these statistical metrics often requires several smaller adjustments to operating practices informed by comparator metrics.

Comparator metrics allow you to compare performance, processes, and outcomes against standard benchmarks or between different entities or time periods. Using comparator metrics to assess performance relative to others or against historical data will enable your organisation to identify the areas of focus and the changes that will have the greatest impact on your organisation's primary goals.

Examples of comparator metrics:

a. Benchmarking metrics:

  a. **Definition:** Metrics used to compare an organisation's performance against industry standards or best practices.

  b. **Example:** Comparing customer satisfaction scores against industry averages.

b. Historical comparison metrics:

  a. **Definition:** Metrics that compare current performance against past performance.

  b. **Example:** Comparing this quarter's staff utilisation figures to the same quarter last year.

c. **Competitive comparison metrics:**

  a. **Definition:** Metrics that compare an organisation's performance directly against its competitors.

  b. **Example:** Comparing market share or net promoter scores (NPS) with key competitors.

d. **Internal comparison metrics:**

  a. **Definition:** Metrics that compare different departments, teams, or individuals within the same organisation.

  b. **Example:** Comparing the productivity rates between different teams.

e. **Target comparison metrics:**

  a. **Definition:** Metrics used to compare actual performance against pre-set targets or goals.

  b. **Example:** Measuring actual CTS for a service against projected CTS targets.

f. **Ratio metrics:**

  a. **Definition:** Metrics that compare different components or aspects of performance to understand relationships or efficiency.

  b. **Example:** The ratio of customer complaints to total transactions.

g. **Year-over-year (YoY) and month-over-month (MoM) metrics:**

  a. **Definition:** Metrics used to compare performance over different periods.

  b. **Example:** Year-over-Year reduction in failure demand transactions or Month-over-Month changes in channel shift metrics.

7.5 Balanced scorecards

The balanced scorecard serves as a valuable tool to steer an organisation by considering the multiple aspects that measure performance across four perspectives: Financial, Customer, Internal business processes, and learning and growth.

a. **Financial perspective**: Tracks financial performance indicators like revenue and profit margins.

b. **Customer perspective**: Measures customer satisfaction and retention.

c. **Internal business processes perspective**: Assesses the efficiency and effectiveness of internal processes.

d. **Learning and growth perspective**: Focuses on employee training, development, and organisational innovation.

Think of a scorecard as a game. It is not just about one score (like in a football game where you have goals), but it is about various aspects of the game, like defence, offense, teamwork, and more. A balanced scorecard does the same for a business – by keeping track of different important aspects and not just one, seeing how well the business is doing overall becomes easier. If you are going to invest in cost to serve analytics, then consider using a scorecard that encompasses the breadth and the depth of each of the perspectives.

The lists of balance score card KPIs below are intended to kick start the thinking process that will help you understand the impact of the changes are making, against a baseline.

Balanced scorecard suggestions

Financial perspective	Example metrics	Metric Type
Transaction cost per service	Total cost per service divided by the number of transactions or interactions with customers	Service cost comparison
Service / product consumption	Sales or transaction volumes per service	Service volume comparisons
Average revenue income per customer	Total revenue generated from services divided by the number of customers	Income comparisons
Customer segment income	Revenue income ratios for each customer segment	Ratio comparisons
Department cost to serve	Average cost to serve for each department over a set period	Departmental comparison
Profit margin ratios per service	Income from services minus service-related costs over a set period	Service profit comparisons
Average cost to serve per customer segment	Variations in the cost per transaction of servicing each customer segment over a set period	Customer segment comparisons
Cost recovery rate	Percentage of service costs recovered through fees, taxes, or other revenue sources over time	Efficiency comparisons
Budget adherence per service	The percentage of actual spending compared to the annual budget allocated for delivering services	Budget comparison index
Cost of failure demand per service	Cost of avoidable contacts that arise due to service design failures	Ratio comparisons
Return on investment analysis for named CTS initiatives	Changes in operational cost after service improvement compared against a baseline to assess the effectiveness of the initiative	The cost to serve business case
Cost of handling complaints per service	Cost of handling complaints per service over a set period	Cost reduction business case
Access channel cost per transaction	The cost per transaction for using each access channel	Channel shift business case
Customer segment transaction volumes and cost per access channel	Transaction volumes and cost for each customer segment by access channel	Customer segment comparisons
Customer segment volumes and cost for each accessibility pathway	Transaction volumes and cost by access channel for the take-up of accessibility adjustments. Examples include braille, easy read & sign language	Accessibility costs
Estimated savings per department from CTS initiatives	The estimated value of savings that could be realised from CTS inspired interventions	Cost to serve business case
Cashable savings per department from cost to serve initiatives	The actual value of savings realised from interventions initiated by cost to serve over a set period	Cashable CTS benefits
Return on investment from cost to serve exercise	The return on investment relative to the cost, over time	Break even & profitability points

Customer perspective	Example metrics	Metric Type
Customer satisfaction score (CSAT)	A survey-based metric measuring overall customer satisfaction with services provided	Satisfaction comparisons
Complaint rate	Number of complaints received per service relative to the number of transactions over a set period	Satisfaction comparisons
Net promoter score (NPS)	Measure of customer willingness to recommend the service to others	Satisfaction comparisons
Customer effort score (CES)	Measure of customer time expended and the ease with which customers can access each service	Ease of service access score
Customer churn rate	The proportion of customers who discontinue using a service within a specified timeframe	Satisfaction comparisons
Customer retention rate	The percentage of customers who continue to do business with the organisation over a set period	Satisfaction comparisons
Customer lifetime value (CLV)	The income the organisation can expect form a customer over the entire relationship	Income projections
Customer segment service satisfaction score	Average satisfaction score for each customer segment	Customer segment comparisons
First contact resolution rate (FCR)	The percentage of customer transactions resolved on first contact, for each service over a set period	Ease of service access score
Average customer journey completion time	Average time taken to achieve the final intended outcome	Experience comparisons
Accessibility and inclusivity of relevant services index	Percentage of the disabled population able to access and benefit from universal services	Inclusivity comparisons
Average customer wait time	The average amount of time customers spends waiting after requesting a service	Experience comparisons
Customer feedback scores	The overall sentiment of direct feedback per department or service	Experience comparisons
Social media sentiment	Changes in the sentiment of customer feedback on social media platforms as a result of interventions	Experience comparisons
Internal process perspective	**Example metrics**	**Metric Type**
Transaction volumes per service	Transaction volumes per service per annum	Service take-up comparisons
Access channel utilisation rate	Percentage of transactions handled through each access channel	Access channel comparisons
Omnichannel percentage	Percentage of transactions where customers are known to have switched between different access channel	Omnichannel use and effectiveness comparisons
Omnichannel percentage by customer segment	Percentage of transactions for each customer segment where customers are known to have switched between different access channels	Omnichannel use comparisons
Data accuracy rate	Percentage of accurate cost to serve data in the database	Accuracy comparisons
Employee satisfaction index	A measure of employee satisfaction and engagement related to their role in providing services	Service / department comparisons

Non cashable savings per cost to serve business change	Number and value index of non-cashable savings realised from cost to serve	Qualitative benefits register
Operational efficiency index	Number of services identified where greater efficiency would reduce operational costs	Forward plan priorities
Staff utilisation index	Staff utilisation on delivering services by department	service comparisons
Failure demand rate	Count of avoidable contacts that arise due to service design failures over a set period	Service comparisons
Failure demand reduction rate	Rate of failure demand reduction because of improvement interventions	Intervention outcomes analysis
Minutes lost due to failure demand servicing	Staff minutes lost on servicing avoidable contacts that arise due to service design failures	Ratio comparisons
Service benchmarking index	Number of services of similar complexity and unexplained differences in costs, benchmarked with each other	Forward plan priorities
Number and percentage of complaints	The ratio of complaints to successful service requests over a set period	Effectiveness comparisons
Channel shift index	Proportion of transactions shifted to web self-service from other channels due to interventions	Intervention outcomes analysis
Completeness and accuracy of cost to serve documentation	Senior stakeholder confidence in the cost to serve outcomes	Quality comparisons
Learning and organisational growth perspective	**Example metrics**	**Metric Type**
Staff accessing the cost to serve analytics dashboard	The number of times managers accessed the cost to serve analytics dashboard over a set period	Embededness comparisons
Accessibility of cost to serve data for stakeholders	The percentage of stakeholders with easy access to cost to serve data	Embededness comparisons
CTS training uptake	Percentage of service managers trained to use the CTS analytics repository	Embededness comparisons
Community of practice take-up	Engagement with the CTS community of practice website / services per service over a set period	Embededness comparisons
Project and change embeddedness	The number of projects and programmes that use CTS data to evidence benefits realisation	Embededness comparisons

7.6 Qualitative feedback

Your balanced score card will provide a strong indication of your organisation's health. To maximise its impact, consider combining this information with customer journey data and stories that explain why things are the way they are.

To achieve this, run regular workshops with staff, dedicating some of the time allocated for training in the staff cost calculation to listen to service delivery stakeholders and record information that might explain data anomalies. In addition to this consider incentivising the use of suggestion boxes to capture staff frustrations and innovative ideas.

Listen to customer feedback and engage with a cross-section of your customer base through user researchers to capture their stories. If your customers use external agencies to interface with your service, capture feedback from these providers and map it to your data. Additionally, seek input from experts in the field, including consultants, academics, and professional agencies. Integrate the insights you gather into your CTS repository. This approach will provide a comprehensive understanding of your organisational performance in context, thereby allowing you to identify and prioritise areas for improvement.

7.7 Experimental metrics

Experimental metrics refer to data points and measurements gathered during experiments or controlled trials. They are used to assess the effectiveness, impact, or outcomes of a particular intervention, strategy, or innovation. These metrics are used for validating hypotheses, comprehending causal relationships, and making informed decisions based on empirical evidence.

Examples of experimental metrics include:

- A/B testing
  - **Description:** Measures the impact of a single change on outcomes such as conversion rates, click-through rates, or customer satisfaction.
  - **Example:** Testing two different webpage designs to see which one is most likely to result in customers seeking less support.
- Multivariate analysis
  - **Description:** Measures the impact of multiple changes and their interactions on the same outcomes, providing a more comprehensive understanding.
  - **Example:** It can be used to understand the combined effect of changes in staffing levels, technology implementation, and process modifications on the cost to serve.
- Cohort analysis
  - **Description:** Analyses performance metrics across groups that share a common characteristic or experience within a defined period.
    - **Example:** Comparing user engagement metrics for people who signed up for a service before a change was implemented to those who signed up for the same service after the change.
- Time series analysis
  - **Description:** Analyses data points collected or recorded at specific time intervals to identify trends, cycles, and seasonal variations.
  - **Example:** Studying trends that will inform staff resource planning.
- Cluster analysis
  - **Description:** Placing attributes that are more similar to each other into distinct groups.
  - **Example:** Segmenting customers based on purchasing behaviour and demographic information.
- Conjoint analysis
  - **Description:** A technique used to understand the value of different attributes in a decision-making process.
  - **Example:** Determining which service bundles are most important to customers by presenting them with a series of options with trade-offs.
- Exploratory data analysis (EDA)
  - **Description:** analyses data sets to summarise their main characteristics, often with visual methods.
  - **Example:** Using histograms, box plots, and scatter plots to understand the distribution and relationships in customer data.

Experimental metrics provide a detailed and nuanced understanding of how different variables and interventions impact various aspects of business outcomes.

7.8 Summary of suggested metrics

With a comprehensive cost-to-serve analytics repository, you can pilot your enterprise using KPIs to steer informed decision-making. Engaging in horizon scanning allows you to anticipate future trends and opportunities, while integrating qualitative stories adds depth to your data analysis. By incorporating experimental metrics and other data sources, you can continuously innovate and refine your strategies, ensuring that your organisation remains agile and responsive to emerging opportunities and change.

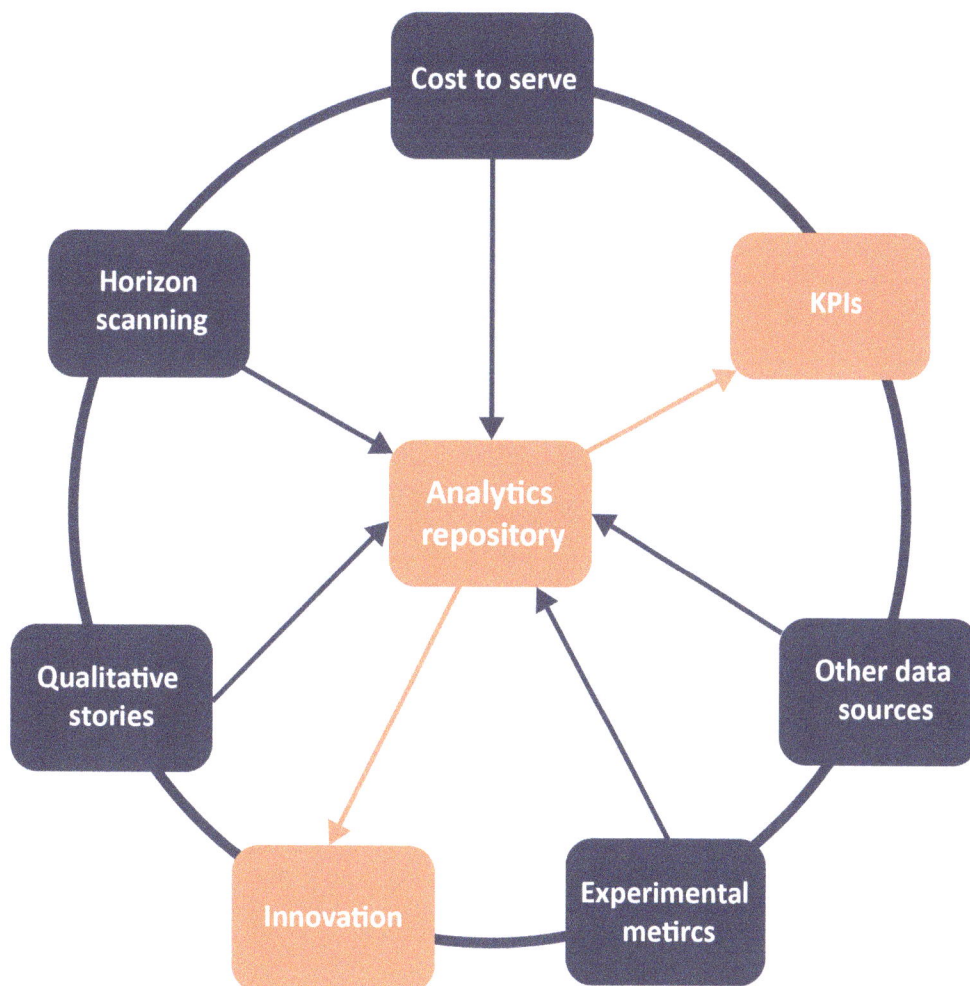

In the realm of business, metrics serve as vital guides, here's a summary to remind and guide you:

Lead Indicators:

- **When to use:** Early in the process, to forecast potential outcomes.
- **Why:** To make proactive adjustments based on predictive metrics like efficiency savings estimates, anticipated productivity improvements and the projected return on investment

Lag Indicators:

- **When to use:** To evaluate the results of past actions.
- **Why:** To understand the effectiveness of strategies through metrics like customer satisfaction scores, cost per transaction, and failure demand reduction rates.

Comparator metrics:

- **When to use:** For benchmarking against industry standards or competitors.

- **Why:** To assess your performance and identify areas for improvement.

Balanced scorecard:

- **When to use:** For a comprehensive view of your organisation's performance.
- **Why:** To align financials, customer satisfaction, internal processes, and learning and growth with strategic goals.

Experimental metrics:

- **When to use:** During trials or new interventions.
- **Why:** To test hypotheses and validate the impact of specific changes using empirical data.

Qualitative feedback:

- **When to use:** Continuously alongside quantitative metrics.
- **Why:** To gain insights from staff and customers that numbers alone can't provide, enriching your understanding of data anomalies and areas for innovation.

By effectively combining these tools, you can navigate your cost to serve initiative with confidence, ensuring continuous improvement, cost reduction, and enhanced service quality.

7.9 Going forward

Making the cost to serve a KPI will ensure that, when projects are planned, the cost to serve is one of the metrics measured. This allows benefits to be assessed against the baseline, ensuring a clear understanding of the impact and effectiveness of each initiative.

Flagship services should not be overlooked. The CTS calculation can highlight areas of the business where staff are over or underutilised. In flagship areas, staff underutilisation can be beneficial if it can be linked to value such as better customer outcomes, higher profits, staff retention, or work life balance.

The ability to optimise processes and shave minutes off average processing times will save cost or free up resources to be productive elsewhere. Failure demand encompasses customer requests or inquiries that emerge due to several reasons such as product or service failures, deficiencies, customer uncertainty about processes, or requests for status updates. These avoidable contacts incur costs for the organisation and can arise from factors like inadequate demand management, suboptimal UX design, or back-office processing that does not adhere to lean principles.

The outcomes from measuring available staff productive minutes per business unit and actual productivity by pay spine point can provide data-driven justification for introducing new operational efficiency incentives and rewards.

By tracking the productive minutes of staff within each business unit, organisations can gain insights into how effectively time is being utilised to meet service demands. This granular layer of data, when aligned with the pay spine points, enables a precise assessment of productivity relative to employee compensation levels. Consequently, businesses can make informed decisions on resource allocation, cost management and the format of staff appraisals.

This integrated measurement framework not only highlights areas where efficiency can be improved but also helps in optimising staffing costs and enhancing overall service delivery.

The important thing in all of this is to keep an audit of each step of the exercise. Who, why, how, what, when, and where, alongside the assumptions that were made for each service area. This will allow the process to be repeated so that like can be compared with like. If the process for collating the information changes, the rationale should be reflected in the audit commentary and the data quality rating should also take this into account.

Lowering the cost of serving customers is achievable through the strategic application of cost to serve analytics, specifically in the effective management of process improvement and human resource costs. By leveraging both historical evidence and forward-looking projections, organisations can make informed decisions to optimise using several variables, including building and facilities management, IT infrastructure, software licensing expenses, access channel costs, and overall infrastructure expenses. This approach facilitates the creation of a compelling business case for implementing artificial intelligence and allows for the refinement of customer experience (CX) design to mitigate failure demand.

The optimisation of CX design not only enhances customer-facing processes but also empowers customers to navigate with confidence. Consequently, customers are more likely to experience satisfaction and less inclined to contact customer service agents for reassurance and clarification.

To unlock the advantages of minimised human effort, it will be essential to capitalise on the accumulated reduction in FTE minutes when they reach a feasible threshold. This can be accomplished by strategically reallocating the freed-up resources to support other areas of the business experiencing an increase in human effort demands or by downsizing the overall FTE count. Ideally, your benefits realisation process should incorporate a method outlining how to convert the saved FTE minutes into either a part-time or full-time staff member, ensuring seamless reintegration of saved time back into the workforce pool, or on the balance sheet.

In addition to assembling cost to serve metrics, you have had the chance to gather additional valuable data, including customer information and process wait times, among others. Yet, it is important not to confine your efforts to these suggestions alone. By actively accumulating individual transaction records and avoiding summary data, you have initiated a pivotal step towards constructing a resilient dataset for service transaction analytics.

In conclusion, this book is designed not only as a guide to integrating cost-to-serve analysis but also as a transformative tool that enables leaders to rethink how their organisations function and make decisions. By leveraging the robust framework of free-to-use tools and insights provided, you'll be able to replace guesswork with data-driven strategies that improve operational efficiency and resource allocation.

While building a comprehensive cost-to-serve analytics repository may seem like the primary objective, the real value lies in how these insights can foster a culture of continuous improvement. The process of understanding cost drivers and aligning them with customer and service outcomes can reveal hidden inefficiencies, improve service design, and create opportunities for innovation. This approach also helps leaders future-proof their organisations by embedding flexibility and adaptability into their decision-making frameworks, enabling them to respond to changing demands without sacrificing quality or performance.

Moreover, the potential to link these outputs with other datasets—such as customer feedback, performance metrics, or market trends—can unlock deeper insights that go beyond mere cost savings. It empowers organisations to optimise not just their financials, but also their customer satisfaction, service delivery, and long-term growth. **With ambition and imagination, cost-to-serve analytics becomes a platform for creating sustainable, data-informed strategies that will continue to deliver value year after year**.

8.0 Appendices

8.1 Cost to serve template for a single service

Use this template to guide the gathering of the data elements, which will inform the cost to serve calculation, and to assign responsibility for data collection to various roles within the organisation.

Service Name/Group_____ Channel Name_____

Calculation	Transaction Data	Channel Data	Employee Data	Property Data	Utilisation Data	Confidence Raring	Data Source
Annual transaction volumes per service	✓						
Average transaction contact minutes	✓						
Average wrap up minutes per contact	✓						
Average processing time	✓						
Average fulfilment cost per transaction	✓						
Annual fixed channel costs		✓					
Annual variable channel costs		✓					
Annual channel volume		✓					
Number of FTEs per service			✓				
Average annual salary per FTE			✓				
Property cost per FTE per head				✓			
Direct employee costs per FTE per head per business unit			✓				
Indirect employee cost per FTE per head			✓				
On-costs per FTE			✓				
Assumed staff utilisation per service					✓		
Average annual productive minutes per FTE					✓		

8.2 Case study 1

A municipal body oversees a parking service encompassing the issuance of parking permits and handling parking fines. Although these are distinct public services, they fall under the purview of the same administrative team. The process for managing parking fines involves four access channels. Web channel interactions are entirely automated at the front end. Alongside parking-related calls, the call centre manages various other inquiries. The parking service is presumed to utilise 20% of the time of street services specialists, 16% of the complaints service time, and 75% of back-office processors' time. For web transactions, 90% are fully automated, while the remaining 10% require back-office processing. The corresponding metrics are as follows:

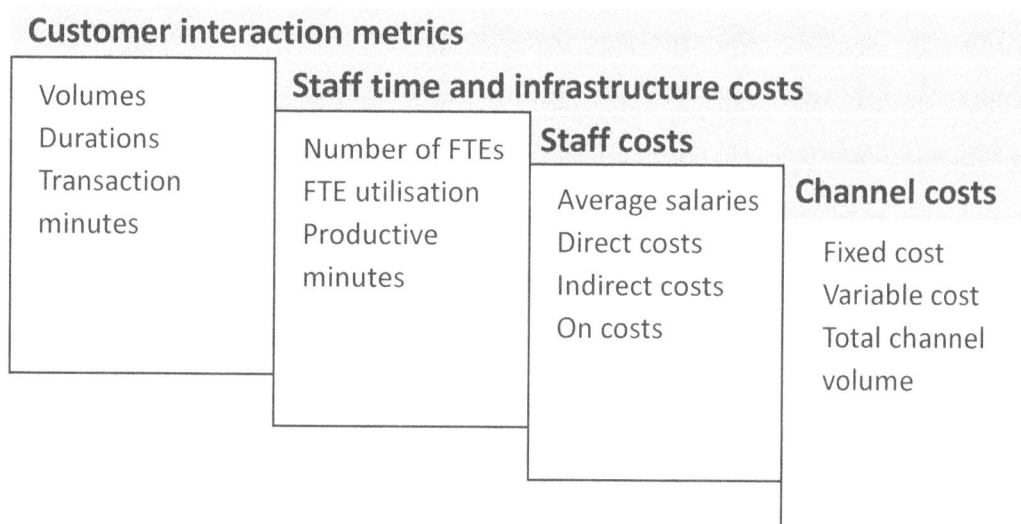

Customer interaction metrics

Volumes
Durations
Transaction minutes

Staff time and infrastructure costs

Number of FTEs
FTE utilisation
Productive minutes

Staff costs

Average salaries
Direct costs
Indirect costs
On costs

Channel costs

Fixed cost
Variable cost
Total channel volume

FTE productive minutes for the parking service

Estimated staff minutes available per annum		Description
Standard working week hours	35	The firm's standard working hours
Number of employees	1	No. of FTE employees in this calculation
Estimated training days per employee per annum	5	Average for the organisation and the role type
Estimated sick days per employee per annum	5	Average for the organisation and the role type
Standard annual leave days per FTE employee	25	The firm's standard holiday allocation
Public holidays per annum	8	Standard public holidays for the country
Available working days	260	5-day week × 52 weeks in a year
Actual working days	217	Available working days minus 43 time-off days
Annual productive hours for employee	7,595	Standard work week hrs × actual working days
Annual productive minutes for employee	455,700	Annual productive hours × 60 minutes

Key	Calcuations	Parking services	Web channel (self service)	Call centre channel	Complaints channel (customer support)	Back-office processing	Total	Data quality rating	Guidance
1		Annual transaction volumes	229,314	54,462	2,866	163,456	450,099	4 Star	5.1 Cost centre mapping workstream
2		Average transaction duration (minutes)	0	8	30	20	20	4 Star	5.2 Customer transactions
3		Number of full-time equivalent staff (FTEs)	0	4.5	2	6.25	13	5 Star	5.3 Staff time workstream
4		Assumed staff utilisation %	0	20	16	75		2 Star	5.4 Staffing cost workstream
5		Annual productive minutes per FTE	0	455,700	455,700	455,700	1,367,100	5 Star	5.3 Staff time workstream
6		Average annual salaries	0.00	32,512	34,860	40,011	107,383	5 Star	5.4 Staff cost workstream
7		Direct cost per head	0.00	6,502	6,972	9,002		4 Star	5.4 Staff cost workstream
8		Indirect cost per head	0.00	10,410	10,410	10,410		4 Star	5.4 Staff cost workstream
9		On cost per head	0.00	45.00	45.00	45.00		3 Star	5.4 Staff cost workstream
10		Property cost per head	0.00	6,012	6,014	6,012		4 Star	5.4 Staff cost workstream
11		Fixed channel costs (based on utilisation %)	92,000	120,000	2,000	361,200	575,200	5 Star	5.2 Access channel workstream
12		Variable channel costs per transaction	£0.15	£0.15	£0.00	£0.00		3 Star	5.2 Access channel workstream
13		Annual channel volumes	1,146,570	272,310	14,330	817,280	2,250,495	5 Star	5.2 Access channel workstream
14		Average fulfilment cost per transaction	£0.00	£0.00	£0.00	£0.00	£0.00		5.2 Access channel workstream
15		Average annual transaction minutes used for service	0	435,697	85,993	3,269,120	3,790,810	4 Star	Transaction volumes x transaction duration
16		Average annual transaction minutes available	0	2,050,650	911,400	2,848,125	5,810,175	5 Star	Annual productive minutes x FTE count
17		Calculated staff utilisation %	0	21.25	9.44	114.78		2 Star	Transaction mins for service/minutes available
18		Assumed annual productive minutes available	0	410,130	145,824	2,136,094	2,692,048	2 Star	Assumed utilisation % of time available
19		Calculated annual productive minutes available	0	435,697	85,993	3,269,120	3,790,810	5 Star	Calculated utilisation % of time available
20		Total staff cost per FTE per annum	£0	£55,481	£58,301	£65,480		4 Star	(Salary + direct + indirect + on costs)/ FTE count
21		Total staff cost per service per annum	0.00	£249,665	£116,602	£409,250	775,517	4 Star	Total staff cost x FTE count
22		Calculated utilised staff cost for service per annum	0.00	£53,046	£11,002	£469,743	533,791	2 Star	Utilisation percentage of staff cost
23		Total channel cost	126,397	128,169	2,000	361,200	617,766	4 Star	Fixed + (variable costs × Transaction volumes)
24		Total cost for delivering the service	126,397	181,215	13,002	830,943	1,151,557	4 Star	Total channel cost + total staff cost
25		**Cost to serve per transaction**	**£0.55**	**£3.33**	**£4.54**	**£5.08**		**4 Star**	**Total cost/total transactions**
26		Suggested FTE staffing adjustment to meet demands	0.00	0.96	0.19	7.17			Calculated no of FTEs required for service.

Summary and opportunities

> **Opportunity:** Customer segmentation revealed that 12% of call centre transactions for a specific service came from individuals likely to be digitally challenged to varying degrees. By shifting just 6% of these customers from the call centre to self-service via the web, an estimated £10,872 could be saved in contact costs, along with 435 call centre hours. After accounting for web-related costs, this strategy could result in an overall annual saving of £9,071.

Parking	Web channel (self service)	Call centre channel	Complaints channel (customer support)	Back-office processing
Cost to serve per transaction	**£0.55**	**£3.33**	**£4.54**	**£5.08**
Annual cost of delivering service	126,397	181,215	13,002	830,943
Staffing quotas	0.00	0.96	0.19	7.17

> **Opportunity:** The web channel currently accounts for 11.8% of non-complex back-office transactions. Automation to remove the need for back-office processing could achieve annual cost savings of £98,051 and annual time savings of 964 hours. Requires a capital outlay of £49,000 for systems integration recoupable within six months.

> **Issue:** The back office needs an extra FTE to keep up with current demand.
>
> **Viable solutions**
>
> 1. Recruit one (7.17 FTEs – 6.25 FTEs = 0.92 FTE) additional FTE to prevent backlog build up or
>
> 2. Conduct deep dive multi-discipline analysis to reduce average back-office processing times from 20 minutes to seventeen minutes. Saving an average of three minutes per transaction would eliminate the need for an additional FTE.

> **Opportunity:** Identify the cost and primary reasons for complaints. Employ a combination of business analysis, UX design and behavioural science to redesign the process and eliminate or minimise the root causes of complaints. If the return on investment stacks up.

> **Opportunity:** Identify the cost of the most common failure demand transactions, conduct a thorough investigation into their root causes, and redesign the process to eliminate the issues so that customers do not feel the need to make this type of contact.

> **Opportunity:** Renegotiate / revisit technology SaaS contracts with the aim of reducing licensing cost and therefore employee cost per head.

8.3 Case study 2

Case study 2 aims to illustrate the imperative of customising the cost to serve approach to suit your organisation and showcase how leveraging insights from the exercise can lead to recurring benefits. Throughout this book, we have correlated operational overheads with full-time employee counts, rather than the quantity of products produced. The rationale for this choice is outlined as follows:

1. Labour-intensive operations: If most operational costs are related to labour, such as wages, benefits, training, and employee-related expenses, it makes sense to associate overheads with full-time employee numbers. This approach allows for a more accurate reflection of labour costs and helps in analysing staffing efficiency, productivity, and workforce management.

2. Service-oriented businesses: With service-oriented businesses, where the primary value is derived from the skills and expertise of the employees, associating overheads with full-time employee numbers can provide a better understanding of the cost structure. This approach recognises the significance of the workforce in delivering services and supports decision making related to staffing levels, hiring, and resource allocation.

3. Stable or fixed overhead costs: If most operational overhead costs remain stable or fixed, regardless of the number of products produced, associating them with full-time employee numbers can be more appropriate. This includes expenses like rent, utilities, insurance, administrative costs, and equipment maintenance. In such cases, using employee numbers as a basis for cost allocation allows for more accurate budgeting and cost forecasting.

4. Emphasis on workforce optimisation: If the primary focus of the business is on optimising the workforce, improving employee efficiency, or managing labour costs, associating overheads with full-time employee numbers provides valuable insights. It enables businesses to evaluate the impact of labour-related decisions, such as hiring, training, overtime, or reducing staff, on overall operational costs.

5. Complex cost allocation: In situations where the cost allocation process becomes overly complex (or impractical) when directly associating costs with the number of products produced, using full-time employee numbers can provide a simpler and more manageable alternative. This is particularly relevant when overhead costs cannot be easily attributed to specific products or when the relationship between costs and production volume is not straightforward.

Case study 2 is centred around a restaurant, where overheads will be linked to each meal instead of each full-time equivalent (FTE) staff for the following reasons.

- Cost accuracy: Assigning overhead costs directly to meals can provide a more accurate reflection of the actual expenses incurred for each dish. It helps in understanding the actual cost of producing a meal, considering ingredients, preparation, and other related costs.

- Menu analysis: By associating overhead costs to meals, restaurant owners and managers can analyse the profitability of each item on the menu. This information can be used to make informed decisions about pricing, menu engineering, and identifying high-profit items.

- Cost control: Linking overhead costs to meals allows for better cost control and monitoring. It enables restaurants to identify cost inefficiencies or areas where expenses can be reduced, leading to improved profitability.

Background to case study

A new head chef has taken over a restaurant. Before making changes he reviews existing profitability. The restaurant opens six days a week for lunch and dinner. The restaurant offers four menu options:

1. Classic British
2. Italian Inspired
3. Asian Fusion
4. Vegetarian / Vegan

The menus are offered via four access channels.

a. Lunch eat in
b. Dinner eat in
c. Lunch take out
d. Dinner take out

Customer interaction metrics – annual meal volumes

Menu option	Lunch	Lunch	Dinner	Dinner	Total
	Eat in	Take out	Eat in	Take out	
1. Classic British	2,696	475	6,819	1,110	11,102
2. Italian Inspired	4,143	848	10,608	1,872	17,472
3. Asian Fusion	3,837	842	9,009	2,691	16,380
4. Vegetarian/Vegan	4,252	635	9,042	3,177	17,108
					62,062

Staffing

The restaurant is managed by the head chef, who employs six chefs and six serving staff over two overlapping eight-hour shifts per day.

Cost to serve

For this case study, cost to serve = the annual cost of raw materials + overheads + staff + channel distribution costs) / annual number of meals sold.

Information from general ledger

Staff			Indirect Costs	
No. of full-time equivalent staff	12		IT/Epos etc.	£1,000
Annual staff costs	£221,000		Channel Cost	£2,000
Overtime, agency staff & incentives	£7,000		Marketing	£2,000
			Accounting	£1,100
Food and drink summary			Payroll	£300
Wholesale annual food & drink cost	£307,011		Insurances	£1,000
			Miscellaneous	£6,800
Total Direct Cost	£535,011			
			Total Indirect Cost	£126,123.61
Annual Property Costs				
Premises, energy & utilities	£105,724		**Annual Sales Units**	
Maintenance contracts	£2,600		Number of meals sold annually	62,062
Waste management	£3,000		Annual Staff Cost	£228,000
Licences	£600		Annual Non-Staff Cost	£126,124
			Annual Food Cost	£307,011
			Annual Turnover	£1,521,009
			Gross Profit	£859,874

The cost to serve: The table below provides a breakdown of menu options, sales, costs, and profit.

Menu Options	Annual Sales	Raw materials costs/meal	Staff Costs per meal	Overhead cost per meal	Total cost per meal	Retail Price	Profit per meal	Profit percent	Cost per annum	Income per annum	Profit per annum
Classic British - Lunch eat in	2,696	£3.80	£3.67	£2.00	£9.47	£16.95	£7.48	55.87%	25,533	45,701	£20,167.58
Classic British - Dinner eat in	6,820	£4.75	£3.67	£2.00	£10.42	£29.95	£19.53	34.79%	71,062	204,253	£133,190.69
Classic British - Lunch takeout	476	£3.89	£3.67	£2.00	£9.56	£16.95	£7.39	56.40%	4,549	8,065	£3,516.16
Classic British - Dinner takeout	1,110	£4.75	£3.67	£2.00	£10.42	£29.95	£19.53	34.79%	11,568	33,250	£21,682.21
Italian Inspired - Lunch eat in	4,143	£1.24	£3.67	£2.00	£6.91	£14.50	£7.59	47.66%	28,631	60,079	£31,448.10
Italian Inspired - Dinner eat in	10,608	£7.70	£3.67	£2.00	£13.37	£27.95	£14.58	47.84%	141,829	296,494	£154,664.64
Italian Inspired - Lunch takeout	849	£1.24	£3.67	£2.00	£6.91	£14.50	£7.59	47.64%	5,862	12,305	£6,443.30
Italian Inspired - Dinner takeout	1,872	£2.10	£3.67	£2.00	£7.77	£27.95	£20.18	27.80%	14,545	52,322	£37,776.96
Asian Fusion - Lunch eat in	3,838	£6.29	£3.67	£2.00	£11.96	£18.95	£6.99	63.11%	45,898	72,723	£26,824.82
Asian Fusion - Dinner eat in	9,009	£6.69	£3.67	£2.00	£12.36	£29.99	£17.63	41.21%	111,351	270,180	£158,828.67
Asian Fusion - Lunch takeout	842	£4.30	£3.67	£2.00	£9.97	£18.95	£8.98	52.61%	8,399	15,963	£7,564.75
Asian Fusion - Dinner takeout	2,691	£6.69	£3.67	£2.00	£12.36	£29.99	£17.63	41.21%	33,261	80,703	£47,442.33
Veggie/Vegan - Lunch eat in	4,253	£4.30	£3.67	£2.00	£9.97	£16.00	£6.03	62.31%	42,398	68,041	£25,642.94
Veggie/Vegan - Dinner eat in	9,043	£2.95	£3.67	£2.00	£8.62	£23.95	£15.33	35.99%	77,949	216,575	£138,626.12
Veggie/Vegan - Lunch takeout	635	£2.01	£3.67	£2.00	£7.68	£13.00	£5.32	59.08%	4,880	8,261	£3,380.54
Veggie/Vegan - Dinner takeout	3,177	£2.95	£3.67	£2.00	£8.62	£23.95	£15.33	35.99%	27,387	76,094	£48,706.48
Total	62,062								655,102	1,521,009	£865,906

Total cost to serve per menu item =   Total cost per meal

Annual cost over previous 12 months   £658,903

Income over past 12 months   £1,521,009

Pre-tax profit   £862,105

Case study 2 summary

In this case study, we observe a profitable business where the new head chef effectively uses the cost to serve analysis to identify underlying issues. This analysis helps uncover areas of improvement for menu items, even those that are currently profitable. By leveraging service transaction analytics, the chef gains valuable evidence to support interventions aimed at meeting customer needs and increasing profit. Multiple interventions can be identified and prioritised based on their potential impact. To measure the effectiveness of these interventions, the chef compares the post-intervention results with the baseline data. The table below outlines the interventions that the new head chef is considering.

#	Intervention	Presentation	Menu improvements	Menu replacements	Changes	Marketing
1	Although the Asian Fusion eat in dinner is the most profitable menu option, the percentage markup is relatively low at 41%				Source cheaper ingredients to increase profitability	Promote meal through both channels to increase sales
2	Sales of the Classic British lunch take out are low and waste from unsold meals has contributed to the increase in miscellaneous costs	Update pictures and descriptions	Source cheaper ingredients and review pricing	Develop new menu within existing theme		Promote special offer for three months
3	Sales of all the Classic British range are low, except for the dinner				Consult loyal customers before deciding next steps	
4	Five meal options have less than 40% profitability	Update meal presentation, pictures and descriptions	Revise menu and source cheaper ingredients	Where sales are also low, develop a new menu within existing theme		
5	The lunch take out/delivery channel accounted for just 4.5% of sales	Change packaging, update descriptions and update photos				Establish a marketing budget.
6	The only Vegan menu option that is doing well is the eat in dinner	Update meal presentation, pictures and descriptions	Source and cost new ingredients	Develop and test new menu offering		Promote through special offers and new loyalty scheme
8	Less than 29% of meals are sold at lunch time, yet the staffing ratio is the same for both lunch and dinner shifts. With prepping for dinner considered it is believed that lunch time staff have the capacity to handle more meals.	Update meal presentation, pictures and descriptions				Increase the marketing budget, introduce discounts for health workers. Introduce new online ordering service.

Utilising insight: a practical example

Expanding on Intervention 5 above, approximately 17% of the company's profits are derived from lunchtime sales, a figure seemingly disproportionate to the operational overheads incurred between lunch and dinner – even accounting for the fact that the lunchtime kitchen staff also prep the evening menu. In light of this, the new head chef has set an ambitious target: to increase overall take out lunchtime revenue by 45%, utilising existing capacity and surpassing the current 2% annual profit contribution from the lunchtime take out menu.

A recent survey highlighted a perception among customers that the quality and presentation of take out meals do not offer the same value for money as the eat in options. Concerns revolved around perceived smaller portion sizes and less appealing presentation. Armed with insights from 'what if' scenarios derived from his cost to serve analytics dashboard, the chef has opted for the following strategies:

a. Localised lunchtime promotions: The chef plans to collaborate with delivery services to run localised lunchtime promotions, to boost take out sales in the area.

b. Upgraded packaging: To enhance the overall experience, the chef is considering a shift to more expensive, visually appealing packaging. This not only aims to improve presentation but also addresses customer concerns about the perceived value of take out meals.

c. Visual and descriptive enhancements: Recognising the importance of perception, the chef intends to revamp the menu by capturing new images of the improved dishes and refining the descriptions. This strategy aims to create a more enticing portrayal of the take out offerings.

d. Targeted promotion to existing customers: Leveraging the existing customer base, the chef plans to promote the enhanced take out service directly to current patrons, ensuring they are aware of the improvements and enticing them to explore the updated menu.

By implementing these strategic measures, the head chef aims to not only meet but exceed the set target for lunchtime take out revenue while addressing customer concerns and enhancing the overall value proposition of the service.

Menu options	Current cost per meal	Target cost per meal	Retail price	Current profit per meal	Target profit per meal	Profit difference	Current annual sales	Target annual sales	Break even sales	Current annual profit	Target annual profit
Classic British – Lunch take out	£9.56	£10.16	£16.95	£7.39	£6.79	-£0.60	476	690	437	£8,065	£11,694
Italian Inspired – Lunch take out	£6.91	£7.51	£14.50	£7.59	£6.99	-£0.60	849	1,231	781	£12,305	£17,843
Asian Fusion – Lunch take out	£9.97	£10.57	£18.95	£8.98	£8.38	-£0.60	842	1,221	786	£15,963	£23,147
Veggie/Vegan – Lunch take out	£7.68	£8.28	£13.00	£5.32	£4.72	-£0.60	635	921	564	£8,261	£11,978
										£44,594	£64,662

8.4 Letter template

Letter from sponsor to stakeholders

[Sponsors Name]

[Title]

[Organisation]

[Date]

Dear [Stakeholder Name],

Subject: Participation and support for cost to serve project

I trust this message finds you well. As we strive to align our operations with the overarching business objectives, I am reaching out to request your active participation and support for an upcoming initiative crucial to our department's efficiency and financial success.

We are embarking on a cost to serve project aimed at gaining comprehensive insights into the expenses associated with delivering our services. This initiative holds significance in optimising our resources, enhancing operational efficiency, and contributing to our overall financial health.

Your involvement in this project is instrumental, and your unique perspective as a manager within our directorate will enrich the process. Your team's first-hand knowledge and experience are invaluable as we work towards a more nuanced understanding of our cost structure and identify opportunities for improvement.

I understand the demands on your time and appreciate your commitment to our shared objectives. Your participation in this project is a testament to our collective dedication to excellence.

If you have any questions or require further clarification, please feel free to reach out to me directly. I am confident that, together, we can make significant strides in enhancing our operational efficiency and financial performance.

Thank you for your anticipated support.

Best regards,

[Your Full Name]

[Title]

[Contact Information]

8.5 Tick sheet example

Name

Department

Date

Service Request Type Key

Code	Service Request Key
1	Booking
2	Application
3	Renewal
4	Status update
5	Enquiry

Code	Time of Day Key
a	Early am
b	Late am
c	Lunch
d	pm
d	Early evening

Service request code	Duration (in minutes	Time of day code	Failure Demand (Y/N)	Observations
3	4.5	b	N	

8.6 Assess Your Organisations Maturity for Cost-to-Serve Analytics

Level	1 - Limited awareness	2 - Repeatable practices	3 - Defined processes	4 - Integrated service	5 - Optimised service
Description	At this level, processes and understanding of Cost-to-Serve are informal, unstructured, and mostly reactive. There is no formal approach to data collection or cost analysis.	Basic understanding of Cost-to-Serve exists. Processes begin to follow set procedures but are still reactive. Data collection and reporting are starting to be formalised.	Processes are more formalised, and data is actively being used to inform decision-making. Cost-to-Serve is starting to be integrated across departments with clearer governance.	Cost-to-Serve analysis is fully integrated into the organisation. Insights are used to manage resources proactively, and the organisation begins forecasting trends and future needs.	Cost-to-Serve analysis is fully optimised, with advanced analytics, predictive modelling, and automated reporting. The organisation uses insights to innovate, continuously improve, and adapt to changes.
1. Awareness & Engagement					
1.1 Awareness & Understanding	Little to no awareness or understanding of Cost-to-Serve capabilities	Initial awareness of Cost-to-Serve concepts.	Broader awareness and understanding of Cost-to-Serve within the organisation.	Full awareness of Cost-to-Serve throughout the organisation.	Organisation-wide mastery of Cost-to-Serve principles.
1.2 Leadership Engagement & Buy-In	Limited or sporadic leadership involvement.	Leadership sporadically supports cost initiatives.	Leadership is actively involved and supports initiatives.	Leadership is fully engaged and drives strategic cost initiatives.	Leadership champions continuous innovation and cost optimisation.
1.3 Cross-Departmental Collaboration	Minimal cross-departmental collaboration; siloed working.	Some cross-department collaboration, but not standardised.	Cross-department collaboration is encouraged and structured.	Cross-departmental collaboration is seamless and routine.	Seamless and integrated cross-departmental collaboration.
1.4 Building a Culture of Data-Driven Decision Making	No culture of data-driven decision making.	Early steps to build a data-driven culture.	Data-driven decision-making is being adopted by multiple departments.	Data-driven decision-making is standard practice across teams.	A data-driven, decision-making culture is embedded throughout.

Level	1 -Limited awareness	2 -Repeatable practices	3 – Defined processes	4 – Integrated service	5-Optimised service
2. Data Collection & Technology					
2.1 Data Identification & Availability	Data identification is incomplete, inconsistent or there are gaps	Basic data identification in place.	Data is identified and mostly available for analysis.	All relevant data is identified and available for analysis.	Real-time data identification and availability across all departments.
2.2 Data Quality Mapping	No established data quality standards.	Initial mapping of data quality, but gaps exist.	Clear data quality standards are defined.	Data quality mapping is automated and continuously updated.	Automated, dynamic data quality mapping.
2.3 Data Collection Standards	Data cleansing and processing standards are not defined.	Basic data collection processes are defined.	Standardised data collection processes.	Consistent adherence to data collection standards.	Continuous improvement of data collection standards.
2.4 Repeatable Data Collection Processes	Ad hoc data collection processes; not repeatable.	Repeatable processes for some data collection.	Repeatable and scalable data collection procedures are implemented.	Scalable data collection processes are embedded in operations.	Data collection processes are fully automated and optimised.
2.5 Technology & Tool Implementation	No or minimal use of technology and tools for cost analysis	Early adoption of technology for basic tasks.	Technology and tools are integrated to automate data collection.	Advanced technology and tools are in place for data management.	Cutting-edge technology and tools are integrated seamlessly.
2.6 Customer Segmentation & Profiling	Customer segmentation is basic or non-existent.	Basic customer segmentation, but not comprehensive.	Customer segmentation is established and used regularly.	Sophisticated customer segmentation and profiling are regularly updated.	Dynamic and predictive customer segmentation and profiling.

Level	1 -Limited awareness	2 -Repeatable practices	3 – Defined processes	4 – Integrated service	5-Optimised service
3. Cost & Performance Analysis					
3.1 Cost Identification & Allocation	Costs are estimated but not accurately identified or allocated.	Some cost identification and allocation efforts.	Accurate cost identification and allocation for key services/products.	Comprehensive cost identification and allocation across all services/products.	Real-time cost identification and allocation, with predictive analysis.
3.2 Ownership of Cost-to-Serve Analysis	No ownership of cost-to-serve analysis; fragmented accountability.	Identified ownership of cost-to-serve analysis, but not formalised.	Clear ownership of cost-to-serve analysis with assigned roles.	Cost-to-Serve analysis ownership is formalised, with regular oversight.	Ownership of Cost-to-Serve is embedded across all departments.
3.3 Cost Visibility & Reporting	Limited or no visibility into cost reporting.	Early attempts at cost visibility and reporting.	Regular cost visibility and reporting across departments.	Cost visibility and reporting are comprehensive and real-time.	Full visibility and automated reporting on all costs and performance metrics.
3.4 KPI Development & Monitoring	No formal KPI monitoring; basic metrics are tracked reactively.	Basic KPIs are tracked, but there's no deep analysis.	KPIs are developed, monitored, and aligned with organizational goals.	Advanced KPIs with predictive capabilities are in place.	KPI development, monitoring, and continuous refinement are automated.
3.5 Cost Performance Review & Adjustment	Cost performance reviews are non-existent.	Inconsistent performance review mechanisms.	Regular performance reviews with adjustments as needed.	Performance reviews are regular, with proactive adjustments.	Continuous performance review with real-time adjustment mechanisms.

Level	1 -Limited awareness	2 -Repeatable practices	3 – Defined processes	4 – Integrated service	5-Optimised service
4. Resource & Strategic Planning					
4.1 Resource Allocation Based on Insights	Resource allocation is reactive and inefficient.	Resource allocation is improving, based on some insights.	Resource allocation is guided by insights from data analysis.	Resource allocation is optimised and regularly refined based on insights.	Resource allocation is predictive, real-time, and fully optimised.
4.2 Long-Term Planning & Scalability	No long-term planning or scalability considerations.	Initial steps toward long-term planning.	Long-term scalability and planning are considered in decision-making.	Long-term planning is strategic, proactive, and scalable.	Long-term planning is dynamic, adaptive, and innovation driven.
5. Risk & Compliance					
5.1 Project and Programme Governance	Project and programme governance is weak or missing.	Basic project governance structures in place.	Project and programme governance is established and followed.	Governance is fully mature, with regular reviews and improvements.	Governance is fully integrated, adaptive, and continuously optimised.
5.2 Audit Compliance & Risk Management	Minimal focus on compliance or risk management.	Early compliance and risk management processes, but not comprehensive.	Compliance and risk management are consistently monitored.	Risk management and compliance are robust, with continuous monitoring.	Risk management and compliance are predictive, with automated systems.

The Cost-to-Serve Maturity Model assesses an organisation's strengths and weaknesses in embedding the infrastructure required to establish an analytics repository as part of business as usual. By identifying gaps between the current state and the desired level of maturity, the model facilitates the development of a targeted action plan that recognises dependencies, addresses capability shortcomings, and prioritises key areas for improvement.

Example Analysis:

Component	Current Maturity Level	Desired Maturity Level	Gap	Priority for Improvement
Awareness & Engagement	Level 2	Level 4	2	High
Data Collection & Technology	Level 1	Level 5	4	Very High
Cost and Performance Analysis	Level 3	Level 5	2	Medium
Resource and Strategic Planning	Level 2	Level 5	3	High
Risk and Compliance	Level 4	Level 5	1	Low

Your Analysis:

Component	Current Maturity Level	Desired Maturity Level	Gap	Priority for Improvement
1.1 Awareness				
1.2 Leadership engaged				
1.3 Dept collaborations				
1.4 Data culture				
2.1 Data Identified				
2.2 Data quality				
2.3 Data standards				
2.4 Repeatable processes				
2.5 Tech Implementation				
2.6 Customer profiles				
3.1 Costs identified				
3.2 Ownership				
3.3 Reporting				
3.4 KPI monitoring				
3.5 Performance review				
4.1 Resource allocation				
4.2 Long term scalability				
5.1 Governance				
5.2 Compliance & risk				

Use the following pages to document the changes you've implemented to make CTS work for you.

Chapter / Page	Your changes

To share your changes, visit www.costtoserveanalytics.com

Chapter / Page	Your changes

To share your changes, visit www.costtoserveanalytics.com